D0070308

THE
BEAUTY OF
SPIRITUAL
LANGUAGE

Jack Hayford

THE BEAUTY OF SPIRITUAL LANGUAGE

My Journey Toward the Heart of God

WORD PUBLISHING

Dallas · London · Vancouver · Melbourne

THE BEAUTY OF SPIRITUAL LANGUAGE: A JOURNEY TOWARD THE HEART OF GOD

Scripture references are based on The New King James Version (NKJV). Copyright © 1979, 1980, 1982, Thomas Nelson, Inc., Publisher.

Library of Congress Cataloging-in-Publication Data

Hayford, Jack W.
    The beauty of spiritual language : a journey toward the heart of God / Jack W. Hayford.
       p. cm.
    Includes bibliographical references.
    ISBN 0–8499–0940–6
         0–8499–1048–X (SE)
    1. Glossolalia. 2. Spiritual life. 3. Hayford, Jack W.
I. Title.
BT122.5.H39 1992
234'.13—dc20   92–32651
                                                 CIP

3 4 5 9 LB 9 8 7 6 5 4 3 2

Printed in the United States of America

To the ceaseless generations of saints,
who have chosen
to welcome all God's gifts and graces;
stedfast in their devotion,
always without fear or apology,
and always with beautifying love and humility.

Contents

Introduction

Call It a Risk with Warmth

I've never been accused of lacking courage in the face of a reasonable risk.

Now, I'll probably not jump off a thirty-meter high dive,

I'll not likely bungee jump, ride a hot-air balloon, take up hang gliding, or ski a crevasse-laced glacier.

But reasonable risks—ones which I describe as "risks which hold so high a potential for benefiting people that I won't refuse the potential cost to me"—*those* I hope I'll always take! This book is possibly the greatest risk I've taken in my years of writing.

There is actually a dual risk present here. The first is that among the many thousands of friends I've found outside pentecostal/charismatic circles, some might feel I'm "pushing." The second is that among the multitudes of friends I have within pentecostal/charismatic circles some might feel that I'm "pulling back."

The fact is that I'm not doing either. Rather, I've simply set forth what I've been saying and doing regarding spiritual language for more than two decades: to focus the simplicity and desirability of Jesus' language promise to us all.

Today's interest in spiritual language isn't prompted by a shallow search for novelty. You'll find it's borne of a desire for God's fullest resources, borne of a passion for anything biblical that will draw me nearer His heart in prayer, which will assist my exalting Him more grandly in private praise. (I am mystified by one critic who begs the real question when he accuses that such a quest is to suggest that Christ Himself or the Word of God are "insufficient" to satisfy the soul. What a graceless accusation!)

It is entirely worthy for any of us to make David's cry our own. Listen! He speaks for every soul who loves God already but who longs for more of Him:

> As the deer pants for the water brooks,
> So pants my soul for You, O God.
>
> Psalm 42:1

My desire in dealing with this theme is prompted by two things:

1. People are interested in an openhearted, openhanded look at a biblical experience of spiritual language

2. It is possible to experience the beauty of this blessing without becoming trapped in current or historic debates or empty traditions

In writing this book, I'm using the more contemporary term "spiritual language" for the simple reason that it's an easier way to describe speaking with tongues. Even though "tongues" is a biblical expression, it tends to conjure up strange images in people's minds:

- Images of uncontrolled speech or incoherent, babbling ecstasy
- A voodoo-like mumbo-jumbo muttered from slightly foaming lips
- Weird gibberish emitted from a stiffened body besieged by hypnotic trance

All I'm asking is for you, dear reader, to listen to a testimony I've been asked to bring. Let me emphasize that I was asked—and notice, please—asked by a publisher not traditionally inclined toward pentecostal or charismatic themes! The publisher's courage in asking me was confirming evidence that a subject which used to be regarded as sectarian has come to a place of broad attention and open-hearted interest among the majority of Christians. Further, beyond this warm, human source of confirmation, the precious sense of the Holy Spirit's presence confirming and assisting me was pivotal in my decision and follow through.

So from whatever point you approach this heart-to-heart, life-to-life talk I've penned on the following pages, I want you to know my deepest desire: I want your heart to be warmed. My earnest prayer is that, in hearing of my journey toward the heart of God, your journey will be enriched and enlarged.

In some way, may this testimony provide a bridge over what for some people have been very troubled waters. That's my hope. That nothing here will become a dead-end street, but instead that this account of my journey may open a highway of expanded understanding. May all of us in all the church become mutual partners in more and more of the good things of the Lord that we have each found spiritually profitable and fulfilling.

Unto Him be glory in the church!

Jack Hayford
The Church on the Way
Van Nuys, California

1

The Beauty of Spiritual Language

The Lord deliver me from the strife of tongues.
Psalm 31:20

*T*he jangling of the phone had invaded the sanctuarylike stillness of our living room where I was at study, relishing the until-then privacy of my place of escape. I rose and walked to the phone feeling mildly irritated at the interruption, having no way of knowing that the conversation to follow would open an entirely new arena of friendship and communication.

"Hello," I intoned, trying to veil my frustration. "Jack," the voice on the other end of the line exclaimed, "please forgive my calling you at home. I hope I haven't interrupted you or spoiled an opportunity for rest." He immediately went on to identify himself—it was one of America's most widely known and broadly accepted evangelical leaders. He explained that he had seen me in a television interview the evening before and had called the interviewer—a friend of his—who, knowing his trustworthiness and the objective of his desire for contacting me, had given him my private number.

"I hope you don't mind," he apologized, "but I felt very constrained to call and to extend an invitation to you."

I was a little surprised. The topic of the interview had been the often-times volatile subject of speaking with tongues; a matter which runs the gamut of being a source of curiosity, on the one hand, to a matter of animosity, on the other. Between those poles, a broad diversity of opinion exists among both participants and detractors of the practice.

He continued, "I'd like you to come to speak at a Bible conference I'm hosting in just a few months. Ten thousand people will be there, most of whom are from a background that has traditionally been either hesitant or resistant toward the matter of speaking with tongues. In fact, some of us were taught that such 'goings on' were a sign of demonic influence."

I winced inwardly even though I knew he was not affirming those accusations. But a near lifetime of facing such criticism tends to beget that response.

"Jack, would you come to our conference? I've never heard a pentecostal or charismatic talk about tongues the way that you do. I'm inviting you to address that theme in the interest of broadening understanding and neutralizing some of the bigotry that exists on both sides of the matter. I think you could help bring a great deal of light and health."

I fumbled for words, hoping not to betray the extent of my amazement. Not only did I feel humbled by the generosity of the approach being made by a so widely respected leader, but I was heartwarmed by the prospect of the possibility he was opening to me. I had decades behind me of having sought to walk with a simple openness to the workings of God's Holy Spirit, always being careful to join those to a steadfast obedience to the truths of God's Word. But it had always been a sore point with me that the experience that I shared with others of speaking with tongues was so frequently distorted as being the domain of either the brainless or emotionally overwrought. Speakers in tongues were often cast as a band of babblers, indifferent to—if not ignorant of—solid faith in God's Word and a sound-minded walk with God's Son.

In fact, my experience of tongues had never been a preoccupying concern in or of itself. It had simply come about as one result of a growing body of experience that had gradually been acquired during the years following my making a simple decision: I wanted to know the heart of God.

By knowing God's "heart" I am not referring to some search for a mystical consciousness or an inner quest for some "otherness" at the seat of the human personality. Nor do I refer to an occult, astral, or cosmically oriented seeking for Someone "out there." But by "*God's* heart" I mean the One and only true and living God—our Creator, our Father—who has given His Son Jesus to be our Savior. And by "heart" I mean what our language generally intends when we use that term.

Just as the heart is the seat of our affections and is used poetically to describe our highest aspirations and deepest commitments, I felt committed to know our Creator in this way (as we say, "with all my heart"). If He has made anything clear, it is not only that He *is* fully "knowable" at this dimension, but He has unfolded clear guidelines to chart the pathway to knowing Him personally and intimately. Contrary to much popular belief and some theological speculation, God is not a veiled Person, holding Himself at a galactic arm's length, or watching us from a distance—out of reach. Having found this out through a profound yet simple encounter with His salvation on His terms, I had years before begun my acquaintance with Him.

It was in this environment that I had been introduced to the possibility of a dimension of prayer which, upon first hearing, I feared exploring. I had from childhood heard of horror stories about "tongue-speakers." A few instances of exposure to the weirdness in unwelcomed instances of fanatical disarray had been enough to stifle early inquiry. But the quiet voice of wisdom prevailed over my fears for two reasons.

First, because in far more numerous instances I had seen the sane and sensible exercise of speaking with tongues. Second, I had also had the opportunity for a careful, unprejudiced examination of the Scriptures on the subject. Thus, I had come to know the place and value of this biblical experience and, when asked, was always glad to speak about it if the inquiry was nonargumentative. So it was with a warm readiness I accepted the caller's invitation to the conference. Perhaps—just perhaps—my sharing in such a setting could assist other earnest souls toward the removing of fears, the dissolving of stereotypes, and even possibly toward realizing the benefits of something I had found to be verified as absolutely beautiful.

It was in that idea, the "absolutely beautiful" aspect of this order of communication with God, that I captured the theme of my message for that evening. Thus, when several months later I was standing at center platform in a giant arena, having been introduced to multiplied thousands as the man who was here to speak on the subject of tongues, I announced my topic: "The Beauty of Spiritual Language."

The reason for selecting that phrase to describe my remarks was not so much an effort at persuasion as an attempt to recast the image many seem to have of "tongues." A stereotype persists, one which suggests that the practice of speaking with tongues is broken from the mold of a backwoodsy tent meeting. You've seen it on television documentaries: a bevy of snake handlers mouthing gibberish while stringing reptiles over their shoulders like necklaces. But that is certainly an image far removed from the beauty and the order which I had discovered during times of private communion in the presence of a loving God.

For many years of my life, speaking with tongues was something too often viewed as an aberration, a self-induced state of excitement—an escape into unreality. And in no uncertain terms some Christian preachers seemed to revel in describing tongues as an experience pursued only by the gullible. Their apparent notion seemed to be that tongue-speakers were people who, on the slightest suggestion, might be cast into a hypnotic trance, a state accompanied by a tongue-twisting burst of syllables more slobbered than spoken, and likely attended by eyes rolled up into a head now peculiarly cocked backward and upward! Hardly "beautiful."

However, on the occasion at the arena, something else seemed to be beginning in the minds of thousands. I had selected the words "the beauty of spiritual language" in hopes that the responsiveness of the hearers might be assisted. And it worked. The overall effect at that event indicated that people could be helped by and to a reframing of stereotyped images of speaking with tongues. Anyone wanting to make an honest inquiry into the nature of such communication in prayer deserves to be assisted toward the image of its beauty. And "beauty" is an idea fully supported by the viewpoint of no less than the apostle Paul himself.

It's perfectly clear that the apostle Paul—not only a university graduate, but one of history's most respected thinkers—saw speaking with tongues as desirable and as worthy of respect in devotional exercise. As the man who acknowledgedly is second only to Jesus Himself in securing the global establishment of Christianity, Paul not only expresses personal gratitude for the continuity and clear significance of such prayer in his own life, but he expressly disallows anyone's discouragement of the same. "I thank my God I speak with tongues more than you all. . . . Do not forbid [others] to speak with tongues" (1 Cor. 14:18, 39). So it was to this apostle's writings I turned to begin my message.

Beginning with words that are among the loveliest in our language, I read from my text as I began addressing the thousands in that arena. The passage was originally to help adjust the thinking of another group of sincere Christians who, years ago, needed instruction on the subject of tongue speaking: the Corinthians. That early group of urbane believers, raised in the classic culture of ancient

Corinth's Greek lifestyle, were in the grip of a sorry distortion of their viewpoint on "spiritual language"; that is, tongue speaking. Even though they had proven readily accepting, as opposed to being passive or rejective as is the case sometimes today, their problem was not so much in their practice as their perspective. They lacked insight on how to allow tongues without losing the intended beauty and blessing of this spiritual language. Paul had begun his correction with the marvelous, timeless words of his ode to love.

> Though I speak with the tongues of men and of angels, but have not love, I have become sounding brass or a clanging cymbal.
>
> 1 Corinthians 13:1

What follows these words is one of history's most magnificent contributions to literature. However, something generally overlooked is that the situation forced Paul to approach the theme from the negative side. Because he was correcting an abusive practice of tongues, for many the sole context of the theme has remained negative. This is an unfortunate conclusion, seeing that the apostle was obviously seeking to *preserve* the practice through correction, not prohibit it by condemnation.

With characteristic apostolic boldness, Paul addresses the ugliness that erupts when tongues are inappropriately employed, when the loveliness is lost, a beauty which might have been realized if the Holy Spirit's intent in the language was not dishonored by the speaker's manner of usage. Thus, in the longest passage the Bible contains on the subject, tongues are dealt with by a man who had to sternly correct ugly abuses. And overlooked, by and large, is that inherent in his goals for instruction is the fact that he valued the place of tongues too much to tolerate the violation of their beautiful intent. A free paraphrase of his opening words above might read:

> If I violate all sensitivities in an absolutely self-centered, loveless display of tongue talking, the tongues become nothing more than a clamorous sound—a cacophony of unharmoniously, shrilly blown wind instruments accompanied by a kettle-battering sound of gongs and cymbals.

The image is dramatic. It is the precise opposite of a tuned symphony orchestra blending its skills under the touch of a gifted conductor.

But I've often thought, "Why should Paul's necessarily corrective approach dominate the definition of tongues held by people who have never experienced them?" Both Paul himself and his readers shared this experience. And he describes his own joyous exercise. If he would freely acknowledge, "I thank God I speak with tongues more than you all," would he intend the words he was writing to become a "souring" corrective or a "sweetening" one? I think an unbiased view recommends that Paul's dealing with the Corinthians' unsavory exercise of tongues was never to plant a hedge against their exercise, but to provide instruction against their violation. Why should the "ugly" be presumed as normative with regard to tongues? Isn't it just possible that *all* the churches experienced tongues, but they did so with such love-filled sensitivity that loveless indulgence never needed to be addressed?

Supposing Paul had been addressing a group who was inquiring for affirmation of tongues and whose practice was characterized by sanity, sensitivity, and graciousness. One wonders if he might have begun with words such as these:

> If I speak with the tongues of men and angels, and do so in the spirit of God's unending love, I will become as a silver trumpet or as a crystal chime.

Having love instead of "have not love" is the point of difference. Paul's plea for order, couched in his own personal affirmation of his practice of prayer and worship "with tongues," makes the imagined likelihood of a positive approach an entirely tenable proposition.

I suggest "a silver trumpet" because it projects a clarity without dissonance and "a crystal chime" because the imagery proposes a sparkling, rainbowlike quality of brightness expressed with a soft and inviting dignity. After all, the figure of a trumpet is used in the same passage (1 Cor. 14:8) as the apostle instructs in using tongues in a way that will avoid confusion. And the figure of "a crystal chime" is consistent with the Greek word, *euschemenos* used in 1 Corinthians 14:40, where a "becoming" practice is urged. The word bespeaks "the graceful, the pleasing, the reputable, the ornamental, of high standing." The "becoming" employment of tongues, in fact, holds an almost charming quality. My experience in the worshipful employment of spiritual language, as enabled by the Holy Spirit's assistance, far more conforms to this crystal chime figure of speech than the clanging gong figure fixed in place by a negative context. And the negative has been made normative by both the prejudice of ill-informed detractors of tongues and by the overzealous, hyperenthused proponents.

I fully understand—oh, too well!—the position of many sincere Christians against the practice of speaking with tongues.

- You only need *once* to have it intimated that if you have not spoken with tongues, then your faith in Christ is thereby suspect of a deficiency—of being of an inferior or second-class quality. Such stupid charges permanently cast any of our concepts of people who speak with tongues into a category concretely fixated in the negative.

- You only need *once* to have been present at a public worship service where either the stillness of pensive worship or the joy of high praise is shattered by the staccato, machine-gun-like delivery of a message in tongues. You never forget it! To experience such a disruptive, unseemly, tasteless explosion is to have an indelible engraving made on the psyche. Tongues becomes attached to an atmosphere more of virtual panic than to one of preciousness.

- You only need *once* to have someone seize you by the shoulders, look you squarely in the eyes and insist, "You need tongues, brother!" Only *once*. And suddenly, whatever reticence you may have felt before becomes steeled to a resistance. But such understandable resistance, once ensconced, is often undiscerned as in actuality being against something *man* did, not truly related to something God has given; something deserving of being tasted and tested on its own merit rather than being dismissed by reason of human *demerit*. The "ugly" in such a moment of crass insensitivity wasn't God's fault, nor are such situations characteristic of what tongues are really about.

In short, here are more than ample samplings of the "ugly" which parades in the name of speaking with tongues, and it's plenty to brace many Christians in a reserve toward the practice. If such things don't produce an outright readiness to run if the subject comes up, they're sure to provide grist for the mill of argument or debate.

Unfortunately, the "ugly" rather than the "beauty" of spiritual language somehow seems almost to be contributed to by the very semantics of the term itself—*tongues*. Our tongues may be a very desirable and useful part of our anatomy, but "pretty" they're not. From our childhood, defiance or brattiness was manifest by sticking out our tongues. Clicking with the tongue ("tsk, tsk, tsk") was for most of us either the admonishing noise of a correcting parent, the condescending cluck of disdain over a bad report card, or the shaming response of a teacher to a poor answer given before the whole fourth-grade class. From early life, and quite apart from anything of spiritual experience or theological concern, tongues naturally seem to come by a bad press. And, irrespective of how delicious a few connoisseurs may declare this cut of beef to be, most everyone I know grimaces at "tongue" as a dinner meat dish!

Helen Pierson, wife of Alby, the former Major League Baseball outfielder for the Los Angeles Angels, tells of a dream she once had; a dream she saw as concerning some people's attitude toward speaking with tongues as a prayer exercise. In the dream, she saw herself in a magnificently appointed banquet hall, as guests strolled among a lavish spread of delicacies being served buffet style. As various guests passed from one splendid spread of foods to another, each one inevitably came to a single table on which a gorgeously garnished tray featured but one item—an enormous tongue of beef. Uniformly, guests would look at the tongue and then, with their faces twisted with revulsion, would turn to a neighboring banqueter—each virtually chorusing, "I *certainly* don't want any of *that!*" Helen likened this picture to the frequency with which she has encountered devoted Christians who savor the meat of the teaching of God's Word, delight in the Bread of daily feeding on Christ our life, and who enjoy the desserts of "the good things of the Lord." But when it comes to "tongues," a knee-jerk reaction tends to dominate the mind-set of multitudes within the church: "I sure don't want any of *that!*"

In sharp contrast to this, however, others have discovered a beauty in tongues and have been able to describe it beauty-*fully*. I was moved upon reading Leann Payne's description of her experience in speaking with tongues. In her book *The Healing Presence,* while discussing the ministry of God's angels as He commissions them to serve His purpose in extending His supernatural grace into our very natural realm, she describes a moment when she was at prayer, a moment when a glorious sense of God's nearness filled her understanding. She writes:

> During this experience, as I continued in prayer and worship,
> I sang in the most incredible tongue, one that seemed to chime

(bell-like) and resonate with the very sounds of Heaven, one that I believe to have been an angelic language. There simply are no languages like it on earth.[1]

She continues by noting how, in their widely read writings of Christian myth, C. S. Lewis and J. R. R. Tolkien seemed to have an uncanny way of portraying these experiences. For example, she notes how Tolkien's description of the glorious singing of the Elven languages seems to capture something of her experience in singing with tongues. The warm candor of her graceful commentary, unaffectedly related as a part of a sensible Christian's prayer and worship, has a way of simply and disarmingly putting away ugly notions of speaking with tongues.

More and more are discovering the normalcy as opposed to the negativity of speaking with tongues. And so it is that I invite anyone to join me in considering the beauty of spiritual language. It is neither to mumblings of gibberish nor to mystical flights of fancy that I invite your consideration. The Bible's description of speaking in tongues is *not* revulsive. When the Scriptures on the subject are sorted out and integrated in a way that shows a whole rather than a partial picture, a picture of the beauty of spiritual language comes into focus. To see it clearly is to see the complete desirability of such a resource in prayer for anyone. To set the "frame" for such a picture, let me make four things clear at the outset:

First, speaking with tongues is neither unbiblical nor outdated. Never have the majority of Christian theologians or expositors argued against the timeless availability of this prayer form. While a diminishing number of sincere but stubborn souls stoutly refuse the proposition, nothing in the New Testament Scriptures restricts or confines speaking with tongues to being only a first-century exercise. Only strained, laborious interpretative schemes can impose such a notion *onto* the text of Scripture. The idea of "passé" or "outdated" or "early church only" cannot be found *in* God's Word.

Second, speaking with tongues is not a transcendental experience. The ways of God in dealing with His redeemed children may be supernatural in the source of His operations, but they are not weird in their ways of working. To speak with tongues is not to resign the control of one's mind or to indulge one's emotions to a point of extraction. The exercise of spiritual language *does* involve a conscious choice to allow

God's assistance to transcend our own linguistic limits, but it *does not* surrender to any order of a mystical, trancelike trip beyond oneself.

Third, speaking with tongues is not a status symbol. One of the most common "uglies" concerning spiritual language is that the sole orientation many have to the subject of tongues is its presentation as a qualifier, as a required manifestation to verify that they, as Christians, have passed some initiation rite. Consequently, if devoted believers in Christ hear this, and they have *not* spoken with tongues as yet, they feel they're being cast in a role of second-class citizen, as slightly sub-Christian—only on the grounds of their not having yet spoken in tongues. Unsurprisingly, they flee the subject, since the very proposition smacks of cultishness and violates Scripture.

Fourth, speaking with tongues is not proposed as a substitute for spiritual growth. As beautiful as an ongoing experience in the use of spiritual language can be at prayer, and as perfectly scriptural and desirable as it can be demonstrated to be, by itself, speaking with tongues holds no peculiar merit. Growth in the Christian life requires feeding on God's Word, walking in the disciplines of His Son, and fellowshiping with His family—the church. But just as speaking a nation's language doesn't necessarily mean that you're a citizen of that country or that you live according to its laws, so someone's appearing to speak with tongues does not, by itself, guarantee that the speaker has been born into God's Kingdom or is living in obedience to God's Word.

I shared these thoughts and many more with that enormous congregation assembled in that mid-America arena that day. Their response was more than heartwarming, and I was told that the audio cassette tape sales of my presentation soared. Further, many of the people present greeted me afterward, expressing their gratitude for having been helped by what I shared, and my host later framed excerpts of my message as a part of some of his telecasts. In all, the event was a marvelous demonstration of what one leader's largess, and his deep desire to see understanding and love fill the Body of Christ, can do to dissolve historic lines of division.

Speaking with tongues—spiritual language—is *not* divisive.

When the beauty of this exercise is scripturally understood and wisely employed, there is a marvelously unifying effect. In the response of those thousands, I had witnessed another case study of that fact. I had, upon invitation, simply shared my own discoveries in the beauty of spiritual language, and a multitude opened their hearts to that beauty. Similarly, by the fact that my words are here in your hand, I must express thanks to you for the openness you are showing to my testimony. Still, I want to emphasize one thing from the beginning: I never did pursue the experience of speaking with tongues for the sake of proving a point or with any expectation of becoming a spokesman for the practice.

My involvement in the spiritual language came about for one reason. It was simply part of a journey I had set out on years before, a journey to grow in the life of Christ and to know the Father's ways. It was on that pathway that I found the beauty of spiritual language. And I also discovered how He has provided this beautiful resource as a strong and tender assistance in walking a specific path—nearer and nearer to the heart of God.

2

Seeing the Heart of God

There is a place of full release, near to the heart of God.

The entire revival service scene was electric with life; I had never seen anything like it! But it wasn't because revival campaigns were new to me.

I was verging on my eighteenth birthday, my graduation from high school only twelve weeks away, and this evening I had scrambled from my gym locker, where I'd just showered and dressed following team practice, and was now arriving just in time to get a seat in the huge tent. Evangelistic crusades—even in great tents, like the one I had just entered—were a part of the Hayford family's life. For example, only two years before, our entire church congregation had joined the thousands who supported the great Mid-Century Crusade in Oakland, California with Torrey Johnson—partner with Billy Graham in the founding of Youth for Christ and one of evangelicalism's most trusted voices. He had preached God's Word with faithfulness, and souls had been saved as Christians united to touch our city.

Other tent campaigns laced my past, but there was something different about this one. The objective of evangelism was the same, but it was very distinct in its style. New to me were a number of things I'd never been exposed to before—not at this dimension! I'd returned, having been there the previous night. For it was here, at this tent site, I had seen something that was gripping me with understanding and brewing an inescapable conviction, one which would bring a life-directing decision before this night was over.

As I stepped into the enormous tent, several thousand people had already been seated and hundreds were still streaming in from the clogged parking area. As the strains of the organ prelude rose, they seemed to beget a holy expectancy, something was in the air, rising like liquid love inside the canvas cathedral. It was doubly moving—seeing the crowd, sensing this faith-filled moment—a feeling compounded by the sight I had just beheld. As I had approached I'd seen many crippled people being assisted to a special seating area where they would be receiving personal prayer following the evening's sermon. Faith was *alive!* You could feel it—everyone gathering did! Something beautiful was en route to happening.

I had been to Pentecostal church gatherings before. My parents had received Christ at the Long Beach, California, Foursquare Church while I was still an infant in arms. Since that time our family had regular exposure to charismatic church life, even before that term was in vogue. However, we had never really settled in such a church, and it's somewhat awkward to admit the reasons for this, because it can seem an unfair generalization. But let me explain. Our family's frequent geographic moves, due to my father's employment, give partial explanation of our irregular attendance at Pentecostal churches (there wasn't always one nearby). But the further fact is that my folks often felt uncomfortable in some of the churches.

They had established a clear criteria governing the selection of our family church home, and these were what made the determination as to where we'd attend. The issues were:

1. Is the Bible preached and taught as the inspired Word of God?

2. Is Jesus presented as mankind's only Savior; His Cross and His Resurrection declared as the grounds and proof of this fact?

My folks were a no-nonsense, yet loving pair who had raised us kids with our highest values placed on good sense and God's Word. We'd been to a couple of Pentecostal congregations which had been home for a season, but this wasn't always so. And that's why I'd been surprised a few days before when they had suggested—with an uncharacteristic fervor—"Son, you may want to visit the crusade services at the tent out in San Leandro."

I had never heard the evangelist's name before, but I did know he was a pentecostal, a fact that made me mildly suspicious but not uninterested. Some of my experiences in Pentecostal churches had bred a certain hesitation, a noncritical, yet distinctly cautious feeling toward this tradition. Even though my folks had come to Christ in such an environment, and I had received Him myself at age ten in the Oakland, California, Foursquare Church, still, most of my years, our family attended other churches. So the awkwardness I mentioned for never having settled is in trying to know how to describe discomfort without sounding disdaining.

Nonattendance *wasn't* because pentecostals didn't meet the doctrinal criteria I've cited. They certainly didn't dilute their convictions about Christ or the Bible. Indeed, it was their steadfast constancy in glorifying Jesus and preaching the Word that elicited our seasons of involvement in one Foursquare Church in particular. But in some other Pentecostal settings we'd visited (including Foursquare), sincerity didn't compensate for a lack of substance. (Perhaps the same could be said in some non-Pentecostal settings as well.) Preaching was always energetic but too seldom with substantial teaching, something noticeable even to me during my early teen years. Services were warm and alive but sometimes tolerant of disorder, and a carelessness in the way church gatherings were governed would regularly become distractive. These are traits more traceable to an era, far less likely to be encountered in today's Pentecostal church. But they explain the tentativeness I've mentioned, the discomfort that had occasioned my family's spending the majority of my years of upbringing in evangelical congregations outside of the Pentecostal movement.

Still, here I was this night, by my own choice entering this mammoth tent where an unapologetic, forthright, praise-filled meeting was in motion—throbbing with the best of the Pentecostal tradition. But tonight—as last night—I wasn't uncomfortable as I had often been in similar settings. Though hands were raised and voices were lifted in audible praise to God, there was a sense of holiness present, not merely one of exuberance. The preaching was dynamic if not also dramatic in delivery, but still the content was so biblically based, clearly presented, and powerfully delivered, I found myself experiencing the real definition of "anointing." For me, the combination of stirring, searching, and solidly scriptural would in time become qualifying terms for "anointed preaching," but right now I was sensing it more than defining it. This was different from the mere drama of style or volume of delivery that I had heard others observe as characteristics of the "anointing." However, as much as these things impressed me, the order of the service and the power of the preaching were not the primary factors that would shortly unsettle my plans and precipitate a decision which would alter my life. What moved me most were the results—the raw impact I was seeing of the power of the gospel. It was being evidenced in two ways.

First, when the minister concluded his message—"Jesus Stills the Storm"—he directed the congregation to bow their heads silently. With a minimum of verbal appeal, aisles were suddenly filled with hundreds responding to the invitation, acknowledging their need of Christ as their Savior. There was obvious care being shown as these were taken to an adjacent tent for counseling and prayer; the sensitivity and wisdom paralleled what I had learned in my own involvement with the Johnson crusade those two years earlier. By the values I'd been raised with, this was the litmus test of a genuine holy dynamic: People were coming to Christ! The power of the gospel's greatest miracle was manifesting itself in the large numbers of souls being saved.

But the miracles didn't stop there.

Following the altar call there was a twenty-minute season of ministry in song; then the evangelist returned to pray for the sick. (I later learned that during the "break" he had gone to another tent where dozens of unusually handicapped cases—some being tragic cases of the grotesquely afflicted—were waiting for prayer. It struck me as remarkable, for attention was lovingly given to cases usually unprayed for by the church, consigned to the realm of hopelessness and often given the macabre designation of being victims of "the will of God.")

A parade of human need began.

The evangelist was seated in a chair where he could lay hands on each one who came before him at the front of the platform and, without flair or fanfare, manifest miracles were occurring. Many being prayed for were so visibly and deeply moved by what was happening to them that only the most skeptical viewer could doubt the reality of God's power being visited upon them.

Equally impressive was the reverent, sensible, and non-intellect-insulting fashion in which all this was conducted. The evangelist was neither coy, clever, or manipulative, but he still showed a gracious firmness, intelligence, and compassion. More than anything else, one sensed an overwhelming love for Jesus Christ and for suffering humanity. Attention wasn't drawn to himself or to his style. He was completely without pretense or any disposition to whip up the crowd to conjure a response. He was moved with each case, prayerful with each person. There was a holy, businesslike way to this display of God's power—and visible miracles were being manifest in a few instances.

This was the same pattern I had seen characterize the night before, so I knew this wasn't a fluke of circumstance. It was a genuine flow of the divine grace of God. I felt I was witnessing something so close to what the Scriptures presented of Jesus' ministry, as well as church life in the Book of Acts, that I was being edged toward a life-changing decision. It would rechart a path I had been planning for the preceding year.

It had been about two years before that I began attending Oakland's Neighborhood Church—a vital, creative Christian and Missionary Alliance congregation under the imaginative and strongly Bible-centered leadership of Pastor Earl Sexauer. The vibrancy of that church's evangelistic ministry was a model for me from my first encounter. I had come there immediately on the heels of my having fully surrendered to Christ's call to pastoral ministry. That experience had snatched me from a spiritual uncertainty which tainted my mid-teen years and now, what I called my home church had become more than home, it was the pacemaker for a heartbeat governing my values and action. I was accustomed to seeing effective evangelism—dozens coming to Christ weekly—and that was now my fundamental motivation for my future.

Furthermore, my pastor was clear in describing what motivated his ministry. His convictions were borne of his study of the life and preaching of Dr. A. B. Simpson, founder of this church's denomination. Accordingly, we not only saw many saved, but regularly saw people prayed for and healed, and the congregation was also taught to seek and expect to receive the fullness of the Holy Spirit for power in living and serving Christ. Thus Simpson's influence had shaped my pastor, who in turn was a warm, ardent leader seeking that path of diligent, dynamic ministry.

Thereby, it was because of my respect for my pastor's sound, spiritually powerful leadership that I had already laid plans for my own training. I would study at his alma mater for my ministerial education, and I'd already been in communication with the denomination's college in New York. In only a few months, following my high school graduation, I'd be bound eastward from California. I wanted a ministry in the Spirit's power but was reticent of what I perceived to be the stigma of Pentecostalism. The die had been cast—at least I thought it had.

But now something else was happening.

Right here in this tent, right now in my heart, something was about to alter that decision and establish a different direction for my life and ministry. That "something" had to do with a holy pulsation present in the ministry I was witnessing, something I sensed to be in rhythm with the heavenly Father's heart.

Everything I was seeing touched my heart because it seemed to teem with the things we know to be true of the heart of God:

• *Here was God's heart for lost humanity.* There was nothing perfunctory about the method of the ministry and certainly nothing peripheral about evangelism's priority. That tent was a gigantic maternity ward where eternal souls were being born again. The reason for the massive response seemed to be found in the balance of two things—a clear message and a compassionate manner. It looked and sounded like Jesus:

> When He saw the multitudes, He was moved with compassion for them, because they were weary and scattered, like sheep having no shepherd.
>
> Matthew 9:36

My parents had relayed these priorities to me—values they had learned from their earliest experiences in the Pentecostal church. They'd met the Savior through the ministry of Watson Teaford. As an infant I'd been dedicated at the hand of this godly pastor. He was a man committed to biblical priorities in teaching and soul-winning passion in preaching, and he was later made dean of LIFE Bible College, where thousands were trained for Christian work under his leadership. These priorities and passions for evangelism, inbred in me as a child and consistently experienced in my home congregation, were being more than fully demonstrated in these meetings!

These two nights I had not only seen a beautiful balance of the Word and the witness of Christ issuing in multitudes responding to the gospel—God's heart for lost humanity was clearly present and clearly primary—but there was more.

• *Here was God's heart for aching humanity.* It is a false dichotomy that separates the needs of the soul from the pain of the body. There is no question that our greater human need is for the forgiveness of our sins. But Jesus' ministry indicates that God is not restricted by a system or sequence of prescribed steps in His approach to human beings. He meets us where we are. He is unhesitant to make His initial approach with a touch to the external of our lives as He reaches to accomplish the eternal in our souls. Mark reports Jesus' confrontation with critics who theologized over human need and yet did little to answer it.

> "That you may know that the Son of Man has power on earth to forgive sins"—He said to the paralytic, "I say to you, arise, take up your bed, and go your way to your house." And immediately he arose . . . so that all were amazed and glorified God, saying, "We never saw anything like this!"
>
> Mark 2:10–12

The whole incident not only discloses God's will to heal hurting people, it unveils the dynamic linking in the gospel which joins the preaching of forgiveness to the healing of bodies. These are not intended as separate ministries—not in Jesus' style, anyway. In His confronting the Pharisees in this passage, I sense Him facing down cowardice and faithlessness which to this day I am still tempted to entertain but committed to resist.

There, in that crusade, I saw the opposite of fearful or faithless hesitation. There was no reneging on the proclamation of God's promises for physical healing and deliverance with equal boldness as His promise of salvation, forgiveness, and eternal life were declared. I became impressed with Jesus' readiness to heal, to unhesitatingly make whole. I was moved by a refreshing compassion for the sick: a passion that melts the theological preoccupation with whether it's okay to pray for people's healing *before* they're saved, a passion that risks instances where no answer seems apparent in order to realize the grace where the miracle or healing occurs. And, inescapably, Jesus was the focus. His presence and power were real, but so was the center point of the evangelist's methods. The demonstrations of power were *not* the objective—Jesus was! And everyone sensed it. Jesus was healing people, just as He did when throngs long ago followed Him to find a loving God who cares so much as this.

At this crusade meeting, God's heart appeared as large as I felt the Bible reveals it to be. And I saw another thing—I was also witnessing:

• *Here was God's heart for practical purity of life.* I can't say I fully understood this on that occasion, but I did "know" it. Because I didn't yet have a trained perspective on the theological and ethical problems related to "churchy" legalism, on the one hand, and "cheap" grace, on the other, I wasn't equipped to make a complete analysis. Yet I did sense the presence of values. The Christian discipline which produces godly character was modeled in the manners and methods of the evangelist, the team, and the band of workers seen everywhere.

Most of us have seen distorted quests for holiness packaged as a ritualized set of dos and don'ts. But there was something here reflecting more of a positive hope than a postured set of mandates. Morning and afternoon teaching sessions issued a call to victorious growth as part of our walk in the Spirit.

The whole atmosphere breathed of God's heart for *whole* people, including their growth in character and purity. There was nothing casual about the Christianity being modeled here. This wasn't a show come to town; it was truth on the move! There were no preachments pressuring piety, but neither was there anything tolerant of spiritual sloth. Everything transpiring simply seemed to take God seriously enough that anyone present would want to walk as soberly with Him when they left as they were when joyously experiencing His power there in the meeting.

This was widely removed from the spiritually bland, superficial excitement sometimes found in charismatic meetings today. I've witnessed the power of God in healing and saving grace in certain gatherings where, at the same time, the apparent glibness and flippancy of the leader's manner tends to diminish the focus on God's character and His greatness. "Glory" becomes a shout or a moment of thrill as opposed to being a manifestation of the *chabod* ("glory") of God, the weight of His worthy presence which begets worship, humility, and holiness. In some of these situations, later discoveries of moral laxity or financial dishonesty have surfaced to reveal that the shallowness in perspective on God's *person* was at the root of the ministry's fall (though there was an honest openness to His *power*). Such things provide believers with many arguable reasons for resisting Charismatic Christianity today. However, that night in the big tent, there was nothing giddy about what I was witnessing. God's holy heart was disclosed in as solid a manifestation of purity as it was a tender display of His mercy.

Furthermore, though at the time I would not have known or used this terminology to describe it, I was experiencing:

• *Here was God's heart for revelation.* By "revelation," I mean the unveiling of the essence of the truth in God's Word with supernatural vitality and enlightening clarity. People *see* truth; they do not just hear it or learn *about* it.

When this evangelist preached, his hearers *saw* the living Jesus! There was no absence of reasoned thought or intellectual skill in the preacher's delivery, but the results were obviously less due to the human skills of reason than to the Holy Spirit's power in revelation. Jesus Christ was *real—alive!*—right there, right then!

Much of what I intuitively responded to in this regard I would only afterward be able to analyze and explain. That evening I simply was sensing this facet of God's heart; it was at a later date that I gained the grasp of its significance and distinctive place in true, dynamic ministry. But I mention it here in conjunction with that night because it was a factor in my decision. The decision I made was not merely borne of the magnetic influence emanating from a man. It was derived from a conviction about how God's message is to be delivered. My "sense" transcended mere human style or personality, for I didn't become a follower of the evangelist. In fact, I didn't even actually meet him until more than thirty years later! But I did recognize a dimension in this man's preaching—something similar to my own pastor—though the two were of considerably different denominations. When they preached, somehow Christ not only was declared, He was *revealed!* I knew both men claimed and taught a New Testament experience of Holy Spirit fullness, and I could see that fullness "revealing Jesus" in a way I believed God desires His heart—*His Son!*—to be displayed.

These matters close to God's heart were distilling upon mine; His love for lost humanity, His ache over hurting humanity, and His desire to reveal His living Word—Jesus—to all mankind. But there was one other thing. That special night, so memorable even now, I knew I was being drawn toward life's dearest walk as well.

• ***Here was a heart for intimacy with God.*** The evangelist had now finished praying for the sick, and the crowd was on its feet. Praises to God were being lifted for His mighty works of salvation, healing, and deliverance, and the benediction was about to be given. What followed didn't surprise me—I had seen it take place the evening before and I was ready.

Without elaboration or extensive exhortation, the evangelist simply invited anyone present who "wants to receive the baptism with the Holy Spirit" to go to the prayer tent after the service concluded. While this obviously was *not* the focus of either the evening's meeting or message, anyone around this environment soon came to realize, it *was* an essential issue. At that time, far fewer evangelical believers than today would even acknowledge the possibility of such a quest. But today, the need and place for a second touch is almost universally accepted in the church. Being filled with the Spirit was clear to my mind as a need—an event pivotal to experiencing God's power in one's life for service and ministry. So it was at that moment that I took specific steps of action, steps which firmed my decision and established my life's direction. From that point in my life the pathway I would pursue was established:

> The place I would train for ministry; which led to,
>
> The woman I would meet and marry; which led to,
>
> The church in which I would serve in leadership; which led to,
>
> The place where I pastor today; which has led to,
>
> An ever-widening circle of Christians I am continuously privileged to meet in ever-enriching fellowship.

It flowed from that evening's decision, which in the final analysis was a commitment to seek an intimacy with God through a complete openness to His Holy Spirit—His power, His works, His fruit, and His giftings.

I went to the prayer tent.

As I did, there were two things on my mind. The first was speaking in tongues, a subject that was somewhat frightful to me. The second was committing to Pentecostal ministry, a matter which had some definition, but right then it was more involved with where I would go to college than how I would minister when I entered the pastorate.

I went to a corner of the tent and knelt at the simple wooden altar rail which had been constructed there. I intentionally avoided asking anyone to pray with me. I wanted to be alone in His presence, to express my heart to God. I began, "Lord, I come to You tonight to lay my life and my soul open before You. I don't know all that my future holds in Your will, but I do know I need to surrender my fears. *I know I need to pursue this kind of ministry*—the kind that meets people at every point of their need. You have allowed me to see a ministry that shows Your heart for the lost and the sick, and which doesn't apologize for giving place to the power of Your Spirit. So now, tonight, I commit myself to that and trust You to fill me with Your power to do Your will."

I invited the Lord to fill me with the Holy Spirit. The potential of tongues as a part of that prospect was, for me, an uneasy one. But I knew two things. First, I knew this experience was scriptural. Doctrinal arguments presented by separate sectors of the church neither convinced me nor dissuaded me. I somehow sensed there was a valid experience somewhere between the cracks of human debating. Second, I knew that both the evangelist and my pastor—a pentecostal and an evangelical—spoke with tongues. I knew it of the evangelist by his own admission, and I knew my pastor's experience because I had heard him on occasions during special intercessory prayer meetings at the church. Neither man made an issue of his experience. Still, it was obvious that each one had experienced something of the Holy Spirit's dynamic, and I couldn't escape the apparent linkage between their experience, the prayer language of tongues, and the flow of power in their lives.

So as I knelt there I was making more than a commitment to an order of ministry within Christ's church, and I was doing more than affirming my desire to receive the fullest flowings of God's Spirit in my life. I was opening to speaking with tongues. It wasn't because I felt a compulsion required by doctrinal interpretation or a desire motivated by emotion alone. Rather, it was because I was feeling the warm sunlight of God's great heart of love for humanity in a way I had not before. His heartbeat was setting a new pace, I was beginning to march to the cadence of what Lloyd Ogilvie calls "the drumbeat of love."

An old hymn sings, "There is a place of full release, near to the heart of God." And right then, I knew I was seeking that. I sensed I was . . . drawing near, my heart coming into an adjusted alignment—seeking to tune more closely with God's. I was committing to a life path of "allowing Jesus to do everything He wants to do." I was inviting into *my* life and ministry the things I saw in *His.* And I was willing to let all His fullness overspill all of me and to welcome that in just the same way the early church welcomed it.

I made myself available to the Holy Spirit.

I had seen the heart of God, and I wanted more.

But I didn't speak with tongues.

3

Love's Language of Praise

Behold, this is the joy of His way,
He will yet fill your mouth with laughing,
And your lips with rejoicing.

Job 8:19, 21

*L*uanne had spoken with tongues.

There's no question that ripples of combined question, wonder, and thanksgiving swept through our family. My sister Luanne had been to youth camp along with hundreds of other kids. Old Oak Ranch, a ministry of the Foursquare Church, has a reputation for offering an outstanding program of Christ-and-Bible-centered, action-oriented, life-commitment-targeted youth ministry. Since the camp was administered by a Pentecostal church, we were unsurprised that the agenda included times of ministry and prayer where Book-of-Acts expectations were present.

But *Luanne* had spoken with tongues. My *sister!*

Until that summer, no one in our family had experienced this. Both Mama and Daddy *believed* it was biblical, and I had no reason to feel differently. But that didn't change the fact that a *belief* and a *practice* are often miles apart. With my sister's return from camp and her sharing of her testimony, a new dimension of perception about tongues had moved into my life. It's one thing to know and have heard of a Bible truth, another to know people who have experienced it, but it's quite another when it happens to one of your family. Here—right at home, every day, big as life, seeming about the same as before, nothing strange, maybe just a little more joyous—my sister: a speaker-with-tongues!

It wasn't as though anyone felt less than accepting. All of us expressed our thanksgiving to the Lord for Luanne's experience. She knew that, and so there was nothing done which would create any discomfort for *her*. But the truth was, the rest of us felt something different than before—if not uncomfortable, at least uncertain.

I sure felt that way.

I wanted to ask her questions. But I didn't, because the questions in my mind sounded like funny things to ask a person; questions like "How did you do it?" "What does it feel like?" "Do you know what you're saying?" "Was it hard to start?" I didn't ask them because questions like that seem to invade the intimate, seeming as inappropriate as though one were to ask a couple to describe their wedding night together.

Further, I felt, well, somehow left out. My spiritual footings in Christ were secure enough that I knew I was *not* less saved than my sister now or less loved by God. Still, a low-grade sense of threat, bordering on rejection, began to creep into my soul. I felt neither jealousy toward Luanne nor ingratitude nor irritation toward God. Rather, I simply had a peculiar sense of being on the outside of something that others were on the inside of. I felt no sour-grapes inclination to accuse or argue. Still, I had a mild feeling of somehow being branded "Slightly Less Than Factory Approved."

Luanne's testimony was radiant. There wasn't anything she was doing to promote a relative comparison of her experience with anyone else's. And who could blame her for her joy? She had not only met her Savior in a distinct encounter, occasioning her experiencing a precious overflow of the Holy Spirit which manifested in supernatural utterance, but something else had happened.

She had spoken Chinese.

Of course, she'd never learned the language, and if she had ever heard it there was no way anyone could attribute what had occurred to some power of suggestion or memorized performance. This order of naturalistic explanation, offered on occasion by skeptics or critics, is well outside the mark of reality. First, they completely fail to grasp the honest sincerity present among most people who experience speaking with tongues. The whole idea—the exercise of tongues, the experience—it's far too holy for such seekers to ever toy with deceit or cheap substitutes.

Witnesses who were present at the altar in prayer with Luanne attested that she had spoken a Chinese dialect with apparent purity. While no one knew the tongue, one there was familiar enough with Chinese to relate this. But if that were not supernatural enough, the phenomenon of language was subordinated in its phenomenality to what was happening in Luanne's understanding while she was praying. In her testimony she later told how her awareness was more of the presence of Christ Himself than of her speaking with tongues. She described how, as she prayed, Jesus spoke to her soul—she knew it. And His words were accompanied by a vision that was indelibly stamped upon her mind for life.

She was seeing Chinese faces—multitudes of them!

This was the most riveting part of her experience, for as the Lord spoke to her and she captured this vision, she knew she was receiving a missionary call to China. She would later describe her happy surprise when one of the altar workers told her someone had recognized her speaking in a Chinese tongue. It was a profound confirmation to each person present, for just as the one recognizing the language knew nothing of my sister's vision and call, neither did she know the language she was speaking.[1]

So Luanne's experience had brought me into close proximity with an inescapably immediate case of speaking with tongues. And as much as I was thankful for my sister's experience and joy, I still felt the question in my own soul: *Will that ever happen to me?*

I can't say that as yet I was truly earnest about a positive answer, for my reluctance about Pentecostalism was still present. I was also having to deal with my own private concerns as described above—that disconcerting sense of being "less." This experience, however, has since then given me a great deal more patience with Christians who react to the joy of fellow believers who attempt to describe their experience of being Spirit-filled. It isn't uncommon to hear someone say, "They talk about their experience like they're better than we who haven't had it." This often breeds accusations of divisiveness. But the truth is that such separation is usually far less due to the recipient's claims than from an unwillingness of friends or associates to rejoice in a friend's receiving this blessing. Why must the jubilation of any open-hearted Christian be ridiculed or required to be smothered because I haven't yet come to share his or her experience? I *can* share their joy—and I *did* share my sister's. But it wasn't without confronting the demon Jealousy that lurks near the soul of the most dedicated among us.

My decision to "accept" Luanne's experience—and joy—probably became more pivotal for me than I realized at the time. I think I began learning from her praiseful spirit, for I've regularly found that praise is the central feature of what happens in the mind-set of the freshly Spirit-filled:

> Then our mouth was filled with laughter, and our
>   tongue with singing. . . .
> The Lord has done great things for us, whereof we are
>   glad.
>
> Psalm 126:2–3

I soon found myself aware of hymn lyrics that seemed to cry out for liberated language, one unrestricted by human limits, longing to declare God's greatness, His love, grace, wisdom, and power more completely:

> O for a thousand tongues to sing my great Redeemer's
>   praise,
> The glories of my God and King, the triumphs of His
>   grace![2]

Somewhere within I was searching for a yet broader confirmation of the experience people like my sister had. Of primary importance was the Word of God, which I already knew plainly allowed for speaking with tongues. Even though some I heard debated the case, it was apparent even to my cautious soul that this miracle dimension of language was biblical. I also knew too many people who shared this experience to believe anyone who mocked tongues speakers. Stereotypes of people seeing everything from the idiotic to the demonic—the babbling to the bungling—were easily dismissed by my acquaintance with sane, sensible, scriptural people who spoke with tongues. From both the standpoint of the Bible and valid testimonies, the evidence was solid. I had also found answers to the question, "Has there been a relative continuity throughout church history of Christians speaking with tongues?" It's been well addressed by earnest students, and the answer is yes.

But the most persuasive factor became praise.

I couldn't overlook the fact that worshipers who press toward God's heart inevitably reach a place of acknowledged limitation. Hymn writers say it for us in a way that resonates within when we sing.

> O could I speak Thy matchless worth,
> O could I sound Thy glories forth
> Which in my Savior shine![3]

> What language shall I borrow to thank Thee, dearest
>   Friend,
> For this, Thy dying sorrow, Thy pity without end.[4]

From the environment in which tongues usually *initiate* in our experience, to the atmosphere which tongues *perpetuate,* I saw it: **At its core, the purpose of tongues is a matter of worship and praise.**

This truth would become even more important to my future journey with Christ, but right now it was drawing me toward greater openness and understanding with regard to speaking with tongues. Wherever I encountered people who spoke with tongues, there was always a triumphant spirit of praise and an attendant spirit of God's love and power. This was still before I had come to that moment of decision in the great tent that night at the crusade. But not long after Luanne's experience, I came to another decision in my quest for the fullness of God's Spirit.

I expected that when it happened I would experience *something!* I expected more than it being an exercise in claiming something matter of factly by faith. Beyond faith's beginning point, I determined to seek something from God that would be a verifiable experience. I knew faith was no less important, but I also had heard and talked with too many people who made a claim but had not had a vital encounter with the Spirit of God. Such formalities are not in line with the dynamic encounters of people who "know that I know that I know!"

To read the experiences of such greats as Charles Finney and D. L. Moody is to find that such expectations are neither carnally motivated nor experience seeking. Just as the Holy Spirit makes personal salvation certain to the soul, I had every reason to expect He would make His presence in power fully recognizable too, that I too would "know that I know that I know!"

There were three primary steps I found myself taking on this pilgrimage. At the time I didn't calculate them or plan them, but they each followed in their time. The journey took me far longer than it ever need take anyone else, for I was an unusually slow learner. Let me relate the steps that hindsight reveals I took on the way toward this dimension of God's heart.

Step One: Invitation

It was always a happy time at our church when the Humbard family came. Pastor Sexauer welcomed this troupe each year and at a time long before Rex Humbard's gift for evangelism became known internationally. The bright music and the warm-hearted couples—Rex and

Maude Aimee, Clement and Priscilla, Wayne and Leona, along with Mom and Dad Humbard—were enough to inspire anyone. But what most spoke to me was the message ministered the Sunday morning of their visit—the prophecy from Isaiah 11:2:

> The Spirit of the Lord shall rest upon Him, the
> Spirit of wisdom and understanding, the
> Spirit of counsel and might, the
> Spirit of knowledge and of the fear of the Lord.

The speaker pointed out how this prophecy, concerning the ministry of the Messiah, is one that the Lord Jesus not only fulfilled, but that He *now* would fulfill in all of His who believed. The truth focused on the manifold fullness of the Spirit and the various ministries He would work in and through us—wisdom, understanding, etc.

This was set forth in a rich spirit of promise, quoting Jesus' words about the coming of the Spirit to each of us:

> When He, the Spirit of truth, has come, He will guide you into all truth. . . . He will glorify Me, for He will take of what is Mine and declare it to you.
>
> John 16:13–14

With this, Jesus not only promised, "What is mine, the Holy Spirit will make yours too," but He gave a direct command to expect and to receive this coming of the Holy Spirit at a personal, experiential level:

> Behold, I send the Promise of My Father upon you. . . . You are endued [clothed] with power from on high.
>
> Luke 24:49

As I listened, a genuine hunger rose within me. The message was penetrating—

pushing past the fears borne of fanaticism which I had seen in my past,

crowding out questions prompted by my sister's experience,

overcoming reticence due to my reserve, such as many of us feel toward the supernatural.

I'd heard all the warnings: Don't seek an experience for its own sake! Look out for deceiving spirits! Beware of manipulation, emotionalism, suggestiveness! Don't let sensationalism about the supernatural catch your fancy! Given the endless stream of such doubt and fear-inducing dictums—however sincerely spoken—there are enough obstacles to block any Christian from pursuing a freely open, fully available, spiritually vulnerable moment in the presence of our precious Savior. But I was *both* hearing and desiring—both understanding and feeling—the truth I was being presented. And when the invitation was given to come forward for prayer, I went to the designated room.

The message had been clear: Receive by faith. And that is exactly what I did. I prayed, "Lord, I ask You to fill me with the Holy Spirit. I want to receive Your power and Your love so I can fulfill whatever You want to do with my life."

What took place next happened so quickly it surprised me.

As soon as I spoke those words, a phrase instantly came to my mind. It was as clear in my mind as if someone had whispered, "I praise You, Lord," but it wasn't a phrase in English. It was four syllables I had never learned (and later, when I mused over them, I knew I hadn't heard them before either). I can still remember them today; in fact, I could write them here, phonetically, except it would seem inappropriate to do so.

I also now understand that if I would simply have spoken those syllables, a more complete flow of language would have been released then and there—a matter I'll deal with later. But that day, I said nothing, because I supposed that speaking in tongues was, well, more a linguistic seizure of some kind, rather than a voluntary point of participation with the Holy Spirit giving utterance. Several minutes later I left the prayer room, undisappointed but unsatisfied. I was very happy to have come to a point of clearly, unreservedly inviting the Holy Spirit to fill me. But I was definitely sure that something was yet incomplete; a language seemed to be present, but it remained unspoken.

Step Two: Praise

My arrival at LIFE Bible College a few months later brought a definite point of confrontation with my reservations about the Pentecostal practice of forthright, verbalized, joyously trumpeted praise. The practice was so common in chapel, in the classroom, in the campus church, and in dorm prayer meetings that I not only quickly became accustomed to it, but I also discovered a number of things about this habit.

First, I learned it wasn't merely a tradition. It is soundly biblical. What I had sometimes seen and wished people *wouldn't* do—hands up in the air, voices speaking God's praise aloud—not only was *in* the Bible, it was *all through* it. For example, the matter of upraised hands. It had disturbed me as seeming arguably to be either a self-centered, attention-getting display or an emotional, unduly energetic, wholly unnecessary effort at "shouting God down." However, now that I was close enough to observe the genuineness of people at praise, I could only verify the God-centeredness of their actions. Their upraised hands were lifted in extolling Him, expressing an up-reaching hunger for more of His life and love to overflow them daily.

Looking into the Bible, support for the uplifting of hands in worshipful praise was profuse. Beginning with Abraham (Gen. 14:22) to David (Ps. 63:1–4) to Paul (1 Tim. 2:8), the Word of God encourages this most natural and appropriate expression of laudation. To my amazement I also found that *both* of the primary Hebrew words for "thanks" or "thanksgiving" (*yadah, todah*) are by their very definition inclusive of an extension of the hand or hands along with spoken gratitude. In fact, almost every biblical injunction to give thanks to God is actually a direct summons to lift one's hands in praise. This ought to be unsurprising, seeing such expression with our hands is actually quite normal among our natural responses. For example, we lift hands in triumphant exclamation over so simple an event as an Olympic hockey goal; we extend our hands while speaking to friends of our gratitude for their loving gift; we wave and smile our greetings.

Finally, I saw it. Readiness to express praise and thanks openly to God is actually the sanest choice for the application of this very *natural* inclination of our beings: upraised hands. How appropriate to do so in the circle of redemptive life, bringing focus to our expression by directing our natural, physical gestures of gratitude to our Creator and Father and to His Son, our Redeemer. When analyzed in the light of the Bible, as well as normal human responses, the only things remaining to hinder my freedom in such expressions are self-imposed restrictions dictated either by religious prejudice, with its taboos, or by my yielding to a supposed righteousness in my adult reserve.

Supported by the truth of the Word and well-reasoned, pensive assessments like those above, I soon relented. I became a praiser of God. I committed to the spirit of praise because of the comfort I found as I learned three things about it:

Praise *can* be properly centered,

Praise *can* remain sensitively expressed, and

Praise *can* be personally controlled.

As these practical facts are perceived and then pragmatically applied, the next question regards how one proceeds. Well, as you might well suppose, the starting point is at the center point:

• *First: Jesus Christ is the center point for praise.* Jesus prophesied that when the Holy Spirit came upon His disciples, "He will glorify Me." This was profoundly and powerfully realized on the Day of Pentecost—the Lord was exalted in praise and in preaching. Actually, the church's first harvest of souls occurred because of questions raised when people praised God in other languages.

Peter Wagner recently told me, "Not until I heard you point it out, Jack, did I see that the languages spoken were being lifted in *praise* and worship." This beloved missionary and professor from Fuller Theological Seminary continued: "I have always repeated what I'd been taught, that 'the tongues at Pentecost were for preaching the gospel.' My past prejudice about tongues was why I had accepted that idea years ago. But that's simply not what the text says, and I'm glad to acknowledge the distinct difference."

What Acts 2 *does* say is that those hearing and recognizing languages being supernaturally spoken, marveled at them. They then declared, "We hear them speaking in our own tongues *the wonderful works of God*"[5] (Acts 2:11). So we see that from the very inception of the church, not only has *praise* been central, but the spiritual language has been a resource for the exaltation of God, paving the way in praise to the further glorification of Christ Jesus, His Son.

• *Second: Order need not be sacrificed where praise is sensitively expressed.* The supposition that spontaneous, voluminous praise must be uncontrolled is not only ludicrous, it is unscriptural. The wide span of verbal expressions the Bible invokes—from silence to shoutings—makes it obvious that varied situations recommend different expression, and that corporate leadership and personal self-control are both necessary and appropriate.

During my early weeks at the college, I first began to discern the distinct difference in the praise offered there from the unpleasant "loudness" I had been so uncomfortable with elsewhere. Here I was discovering both a creativity—not just a monotonous noisiness. Praise found a wide variety of expressions by worshipers—from whispered murmurs of worship, to loud praises, to applause, depending on what the situation recommended.

Whereas one side of my church background had virtually ordered ritual silence, with equal religiousness the other had seemed to sanctify noise for its own sake. Now I was finding that the beauty was in the blending. This invited a new freedom in praise, to exercise the whole spectrum of potential praise participation without a sense of either cool restriction or unbridled license. In other words, just as people weren't being stifled, neither were they glibly loosed to a pretentious un-governedness. Guidelines in the Word and the wisdom of gracious lead-ership kept order in the services. And with direct reference to speaking with tongues, public praise in those languages in the company of un-believers was systematically avoided because the Bible taught such control (1 Cor. 14:16–17, 23).

• *Third: The God-given power of our will is never intended to be out of control.* It was in this light that the relationship between praise, spiritual language, and the choice involved in speaking both became clear to me. In writing the Corinthians, Paul says,

> I will pray with the spirit, and I will also pray with the understand-ing. I will sing with the spirit, and I will also sing with the under-standing.
>
> 1 Corinthians 14:15

His direct "I will" asserts both (1) his decisiveness to employ spiritual language in his personal praise—spoken or sung; and (2) his determi-nation to do so as readily as he would speak or sing when he under-stands the words used.

Paul firmly states, in effect: "I'm fully submitted to the Holy Spirit in this exercise, but I'm still the one who chooses when and where to speak or sing in my spiritual language—in other tongues." A few verses later the same concept is brought into application. Advancing his in-structions that order be insisted on in the corporate gatherings of the congregation, he writes: "The spirits of the prophets are subject to the prophets" (1 Cor. 14:32). The role of each person in helping maintain order is being underscored, as the apostle essentially says: "*You* are the ones who determine *if* and *when* you speak. Don't blame the Holy Spirit if tasteful order is violated in your meetings!"

Observing these scriptural guidelines in no way minimizes the supernatural source of Holy-Spirit-prompted speech, whether it is anointed preaching, a timely word of witness, a joyous exclamation of praise, or an expression spoken in other tongues. The Bible teaches that while God gives us the reasons *for* praise, the power *to* praise, and the call *unto* praise, we are the ones who make the decision as to when, how, and where to do it.

The climate of this understanding opened my way to release in receiving the privileged resource and beauty of spiritual language. It wasn't until these praise principles became clear that I finally spoke with tongues. The last point—*you* decide when and where—took so long for me to understand. But when I did, the freedom to speak finally came.

Step Three: Decision

Those four syllables were still in my mind—they'd never gone away and they'd never been spoken. To some people that may seem a strange fact, but I had now restrained from speaking them for more than three years. And not only did I withhold speaking those four syllables, but now there were more.

Perhaps I should be more hesitant to tell this part of my testimony, because I honestly don't want anyone to presume that I think that everyone who speaks with tongues either has begun or will begin the same way I did. But I have found that what I *did* experience has been confirmed by others frequently enough to say that my experience isn't unusual. So I offer this witness hoping it may assist your understanding, but also presuming you know it is not intended to be a controlling standard or a perfect model.

God is endlessly creative in His ways. While we do share certain things as being the same in our community of Christian experience, there is nonetheless a matchless variety of ways that Jesus Himself ministers the Holy Spirit's fullness to His own dear ones. *He* is the Baptizer, and the privilege of *how* He will minister to you is His alone. Trust Him.

I finally did.

It isn't that I hadn't trusted Him before. Prior to that May evening, during my junior year of college, I'd obviously already trusted Christ as my Savior. For more than a decade I'd known His love and was at rest in His saving work, finished for me at the Cross. But what awaited now was to trust Him in the unique matter of speaking with tongues.

During the intervening three years,
Since that Sunday morning at church when I *invited* Jesus to
fill me overflowingly,
Following my *commitment* to Spirit-filled ministry,
During which time I'd learned a pathway of *praise* at college,
a slow progress had been realized.

But *now*—now the moment of *decision* had come. The decision involved a fact I've seldom related: The number of syllables had increased! I hesitate telling this because inevitably someone falls into the process of skeptically analyzing my experience without realizing I had already done that all along. I knew I hadn't conjured up, overheard, or worked at mentally forming these words. My own reverence for what I was expecting from God disallowed such human concoctings. Still, this expansion to about a dozen syllables, which virtually formed a complete phrase, had occurred in three distinct steps on two separate occasions about a year apart and had been added to the original instance I described.

Two things precipitated my prayerfully speaking this phrase: understanding and faith. I learned that the experience of spiritual language involves a decision *to* speak, and this helped me past the notion that some divine seizure of my tongue, some "supernatural jiggling" would take place. In Acts 2:4, which is the first time anyone ever actually spoke with tongues, this key text assists us in understanding the link between the *miracle* of the language and the *mind-set* to speak in response.

> And they were all filled with the Holy Spirit and began to speak with other tongues, as the Spirit gave them utterance.

The verb "they began" is pointed in its timing—aorist being the Greek tense. The grammatical form makes the statement clear—"At this point *they* (the people being filled) began (as a participative response) to speak with tongues." The linguistic miracle is shown in the verb in the phrase "as the Spirit *gave*." The tense is imperfect, which grammatically allows this paraphrase: "The Spirit was continuously giving them what they were speaking out loud."

It's also a striking fact that the verb *apophthegomai* ("utterance") is used; a word in common Greek usage which not only described outspoken, declarative speech, but which was used for speech thought to be motivated by a divine, prophetic impulse. So Paul's explanation that Holy-Spirit-inspired speech is still only spoken by the speaker's choice, and the fact that that's the way Pentecost was, both released me to decide: I *will* speak! It wasn't a presumption born of enthusiasm, but an obedience born of faith.

The role of faith in receiving anything from God is paramount. At this moment my faith had been stirred by a message brought by Jerry Jensen. Jerry, then in youth work but later to become the editor of the globe-encircling *Voice* magazine, had spoken on the text: "Take up your bed and walk!" (John 5:8). I had been a part of the platform team that evening, and following my part in the service I had taken a seat in the front row of the congregation. God's Word peeled back all hesitation as the message simply asked: "If you haven't received from God what His promises provide, why not!?" I took action.

I didn't stop then to analyze all the factors that had brought me to this moment. The decision long past, the praise since learned—these weren't on my mind. In fact, the faith I sensed was not attended by sentiment or emotion. It was almost embarrassingly matter of fact. Expressions of praise-filled emotion, as well as impassioned prayer, had been a part of numerous occasions before, but now I simply said: "Lord, I've been hesitant to speak these words for all this time, even though I know and believe they have been prompted by Your Holy Spirit. But now I am going to speak them. In doing so, I bring myself under the power of the Blood of Your Cross, to assure that nothing I do would in any way displease You or be self-deceptive. If I speak those words and nothing more occurs, I'll rest the matter with you *in* faith. But if, as I believe will be the case—if I *do* continue to speak with tongues beyond these few syllables—I ask this one thing: I ask that it continue as a part of my daily life and not simply end with this single event." Then I said, "In Jesus' Name, I speak these words . . ."

I began to speak with tongues.

I spoke those few syllables . . . and continued beyond them. I went on into an extended season of prayer in the exercising of a new language enabled by the Holy Spirit. (Interestingly, I never again spoke those original syllables.) There on my knees before God that spring evening, I worshiped with thankfulness, both in English and in a language (or languages) I had never learned.

And I wept. Not profusely, but with moistened eyes I expressed my praise to God for my finally having come to this point of release. I was happy—not because of tongues, but because of Jesus! I knew He had patiently brought me *beyond* doubt and fear, *around* tradition, *past* sensation, and *unto* Himself.

I had finally broken into an arena of privilege so openly available to any Christian, I wondered why I had been so slow to enter. But in another sense, I think I actually knew why. My slowness of response was related to the same things that hinder a host of us who love Christ with all our hearts.

- We reject simplistic categories which seem to suggest our experience with God is invalidated without tongues.
- We suspect manipulative means which goad toward tongues without focusing on Christ Himself.
- We doubt the practicality of having an emotional experience if it doesn't contribute to some lasting benefit or worth on the long road of Christian discipleship.

Those, among other issues, had now been surmounted. I had not only sensed that Jesus Christ had filled me with the Holy Spirit, but I had also experienced a release into a beautiful language of praise and prayer. I had also asked the Lord to allow this to be more than a moment's experience, and it didn't take long to find that request answered.

When I arose the next morning, I went into the living room of Anna's and my small apartment. We'd been married about a year and were now planning for our pastoral beginnings, which were about to launch in just a few months. When I had returned home the night before, she had rejoiced with me when I had told her what had happened. But now, there on my knees in my private place of morning devotion, I began with my usual prayer pattern. A few minutes later, I simply said, "Lord Jesus, last night You began a good work of a new kind in me. I've asked You to continue it until You come again. So now, I invite the Holy Spirit *today* to enable me afresh—and ongoingly."

And the language flowed simply, "naturally supernatural" as someone described it. And best of all, I worshiped God—perhaps not *actually* closer to His heart than ever before, but certainly with a *liberty* of expressing my love for Him which was newer and fuller than I'd ever known.

4

Though I Speak with Tongues

Love suffers long and is kind; . . . does not parade itself, is not puffed up; does not behave rudely, . . . rejoices in the truth; bears all things, believes all things, hopes all things, endures all things.

1 Corinthians 13:4–7

*H*ave you ever met Adrian Plass? I did, about four years ago, through "Diary"—a sometimes screamingly funny, yet peculiarly poignant exposure of the idiosyncratic efforts of a "renewal Christian" at navigating his new call to supernatural living.

The Sacred Diary of Adrian Plass (Age 37 1/2) is the imaginative creation of the real Adrian Plass, an English author who also hosts a late-night religious television program in Britain. Plass, as the Diary's slightly-bewildered-but-always-lovingly-sincere seeker, relates his day-to-day quest for a spiritual life in the real not-so-conducive-to-spiritual-living world. He describes his dilemma with such honest-to-Godness that you are both touched by the semipathos of his true heart cry and moved to laughter's tears reading of his efforts at being a "truly Spirit-filled Christian." You end up loving this character, recognizing your own partnership in his at-times-befuddled journey.

The distinguishing trait of Adrian Plass is by no means his superiority of spirituality. It's more simply in his pure but puzzled desire to integrate the call to a contemporary power-filled life into the ordinariness of his mundane environment. The realities we all face, as well as frustrations felt in our hope for supernature amid the common place is, for example, expressed in this excerpt. This hilarious clip captures the mood of the "Diary," as we encounter Adrian's inquiring soul raising the earnest question every Christian has asked at some time: "How do I know God's voice, or leading, or direction?"

Sunday February 16th
  Wish there was an easy way of knowing when thoughts are just thoughts, and not messages from God. Had a thought just after quiet-time today. Just came into my head suddenly.
  "Buy a tree-frog and call it Kaiser Bill."
  Sounds utterly absurd, but why should a thought like that just pop up from nowhere? Was going to tell Anne and Gerald but decided (especially after yesterday) I would just be inviting ridicule, like Richard and his impaled jellyfish. I've written the words down on a piece of paper, and put it in the inside pocket of my second best suit. After all, you never know![1]

I suppose I enjoy Adrian's diary so much because, as you read, you end up with the description of a good-hearted, well-intended, candidly honest, sincerely desirous-to-please-God Christian. And in the end, Adrian proves to be no fool, but a servant-hearted saint who seems to be somewhat adequately blundering his way to heaven's ultimate glory along a pathway of genuine efforts at biblical faith and discipline.

He frequently comes to mind when I look around at the mixture of earnest believers I know who, like me, truly want to "pursue the possibilities" of supernatural living.

We aren't weird.

Honestly.

In fact, believers like this aren't even dangerous. Because the realism that dominates every committed Christian's life—be they charismatic or otherwise—finally keeps us from the bizarre or the mystical murkiness that muddies the record. Unfortunately, a handful of fanatics, however rare their actual appearance, is all it takes to create the stereotypes which are seized with glee by any who question or oppose another sector of the church community. Because of the fact that somewhere, sometime, someone "screamed in tongues at the concert," or, "He started shouting praise to God in the middle of the prayer over the bride and groom at today's wedding!" the caricature of a charismatic as being "a little more than a half-bubble off-center" lurks in the minds of multitudes.

For years I've wanted to write a book entitled, *What IS Charismatic and What ISN'T*. But I've not done it for two reasons. First, because no one assigned me the role of being the final interpreter or definer of the movement. Second, because I would probably end up drawing fire from friends I was hoping to defend, as surely as I would likely find objections from committed opponents to *anything* charismatic. Of course, my reason for wanting to pursue such a subject is that I become so weary of the rejection as well as the caricaturing that attends some circles because of the stereotypical images which seem indelibly ingrained.

It only needs to happen to you once, and you know you've been initiated! I don't mean, speak with tongues—I mean, be *avoided* because you do, or "tastefully withdrawn from," or when you're not there set aside as a consideration for the position, or your book or broadcast dismissed as "not to be sold in this store," or "not aired over this station."

It only has to happen once, and you remember.

I was at a national gathering of evangelical leaders, one which by invitation included the whole spectrum, from charismatics and pentecostals through non-charismatics, traditional evangelicals, to mainline Protestants. I was young in the ministry, still unoriented to the nuances of interdenominational gatherings, so I wasn't ready for what happened the moment I answered a well-known Christian's inquiry following our self-introductions. "Jack—It's good to meet you. Where do you minister?"

"I'm in youth ministry with the Foursquare Church."

Sudden silence.

The hand gripping mine went limp as the eyes above a wan smile before me turned to find somewhere else in the room to go.

A sudden "Excuse me," and I'm standing there . . . alone.

The bad news is the scenario isn't imagined, but real. The good news is that it's far less likely to happen among the broad mix of Christ's Body today than when the icy moment slapped my face those many years ago.

The memory's pain has long since been handled; the unwitting injurer of my soul forgiven, the frequency of such occurrences vastly reduced. But the sobering fact is that a peculiar thing happens in some people's minds if they know or think you're "one of those," someone who speaks with tongues. To observe as much isn't a surrender to paranoia, nor is it to deny that given another gathering and a different exchange in conversation the same thing might be done by a charismatic to a *non*-charismatic.

The whole matter of defining *charismatic* has become a bit muddled of late. There are any number of things that caricature this sector of Christianity. But like most caricatures, aside from the slightly comic exaggeration of features, there is the usual overlooking of significant factors. The features are generally rather superficial to the substance that constitutes the factors which most govern the individual or group. To cartoon an athlete's muscles overlooks the fact of his academic achievements. To draw the operatic mezzo-soprano's bustiness may be a clever identifier of her person, but it probably misses capturing the genuineness of her personality, not to mention the scope of her musical talent.

Allow me the privilege of speaking for most people I know who speak with tongues. They aren't compulsive wavers of hands just because a song of praise is sung. They likely may raise them, but it isn't a written rule of being charismatic. Neither are they characterized by the seeming mystical otherworldliness you might have encountered in some sincere but misguided saint who claimed a charismatic experience.

Paul said, "Though I speak with the tongues of men and angels and have not love," and thereby approached the subject in a corrective, yet constructive way. But again, I cannot help but wonder if the same man, had we the opportunity to talk with him further as to the beauty and the blessing *when we are loving,* would not affirm that people who speak with tongues are not merely tongue speakers. There is so much more about us (just as there was so much more about Paul, the self-announced all-time speaker with tongues).

For my own part—and I think I *do* represent millions of ordinary Christians who are seeking to walk in biblically charted, extra-ordinary paths of life, love, and service—let me tell a little more about myself. As one to whom the spiritual language has been a boon and blessing in drawing me closer to God's heart, I am more than just a tongue speaker. There are a number of other traits that ought to be added; traits which I think are equally true of millions of Christians who share this experience.

• Though I speak with tongues, *I am an intelligent person.* At the risk of those words being misconstrued as suggesting the proposition that I see myself as "intellectual," I start here. *Intelligent;* that is, reasonable, reasoning, coherent, rational—as opposed to mindless, scatterbrained, or gullible. In our Western world, the intellect is often bowed to before any other attribute of personality. But I'm not appealing to an IQ status or the ability to manipulate computer programs, to quote Chaucer by the yard, or to explain the theory of relativity. I'm simply affirming that though I speak with tongues, I haven't taken leave of my mental faculties.

Nor do I take leave of them *when* I speak with tongues.

It is a mistake in nomenclature that some writers have described speaking with tongues as irrational speech. Worse yet, many have proposed it is not a language, but only garbled speech—gibberish. To pass such judgment is to presume the observer knows every one of the earth's nearly six thousand tongues (not to mention the possibility that beyond this planet a few other heavenly languages may be spoken). To indict tongues with the charge of gibberish—*ever*—is also to acknowledge one's ignorance of the innumerable times that tongues spoken by Holy-Spirit-filled people have been recognized by hearers.

The very exercise of tongues is an intelligent act; not that the language is known, but that . . .

the choice to speak is known (1 Cor. 14:15),

the Person being spoken to is known (1 Cor. 14:2), and

the content of what is spoken is sometimes perceived after the fact (1 Cor. 14:13).

This is *not* irrational speech as some have referred to it. The spiritual language may be described as *supra*rational, because it does *exceed* the limits of the mind's unaided capacities, but it is *not* an aberrant or ignorant exercise. Because a tongue may be *incomprehensible* to the human mind does not mean one is *incoherent* in his or her exercise of the spiritual language. The Word of God says, with reference to speaking in other languages, "None of them is without significance" (1 Cor. 14:10). My intelligence may not be ministered to when I speak with tongues, but neither is it violated. Though I speak with tongues, I am not rendered less than an intelligent person. And,

• Though I speak with tongues, *I am a sensible person.* By "sensible," I mean a person of practical good sense; to be reasonable and resistant to the absurd, foolish, or the fatuous. I could only wish that *every* person who has *ever* spoken with tongues realized that to do so was not an invitation to "la-la" land. God hasn't ordained that our experiences in the supernatural are an exit pass from the realm of the natural, the mundane, or the sensibly practical. I've encountered only a few who supposed this, but it's doubly painful each time. It's painful because of the instances of raw inanity or outright stupidity which have masqueraded in the name of the Holy Spirit, and it's painful because once such things take place, they seem to become indelibly etched in the memory of all who witness it or hear about it. Dumb things done by a charismatic are usually chalked up to his or her being a tongues speaker, rather than noting that the same person *sans tongues* would probably have done the same dumb thing!

To speak with tongues does not constitute a requirement to resign your senses any more than it requires trading in your brain to exercise faith in the existence of God. And yet there are enough cases of tongue speakers who have sacrificed basic common sense in their application of their spiritual language that we need to make these observations. But because a charismatic moment prompted some person's wildest imagination toward even wilder action, doesn't mean either you or I are mandated to do the same for having received the blessing of prayer's spiritual language.

However, there *is* an aspect of this subject which deserves a fairer evaluation than is often granted. It's worth noting that some newly Spirit-filled Christians *do appear* to have suddenly changed in their emotional responses or their general outlook on life. And it's understandable that an unconverted friend, relative, or a doctrinaire critic of charismatic experience may be disturbed by this change. In many of these cases the problem isn't with the newly dubbed charismatic, but with those who are shaken by the newfound freedom, the unrepressed joy, and the childlike openness of their formerly "controlled" friend. The accusation that a spiritually liberated person may have lost control isn't always deserved. I've seen both:

- The person whose charismatic experience has been made an excuse or an explanation for irresponsibility or just plain goofiness; in contrast with,

- The person whose charismatic experience has birthed a new freedom in personal behavior, manifesting a joy borne of the release from fears, destructive habits or repressing influences out of the past.

Sensibility allows for the distinguishing between the two: (1) graciously acknowledging a person's *real* newfound liberty, as well as (2) appropriately correcting instances when someone's foolishness parades as spirituality. Though I speak with tongues I am not rendered less than a sensible person. And,

• Though I speak with tongues, *I am a fallible person*. Perhaps few accusations are more unfounded than the oft-quoted criticism of people who claim a new Spirit-fullness, or entry into an experience of speaking with tongues: "They think they're better than everyone else!" Within the circle of my associations, nothing could be further from the real feelings of the Spirit-filled Christian.

A more accurate description of our feelings was summarized by a man I heard relating his experience in the Holy Spirit to a gathering of two thousand or more fellow Lutherans who had invited his testimony. He said,

> To those who say my expanded joy in Christ is an innuendo suggesting myself "better" than they, I want to fully deny it. However, along with many of you—my friends who have come to share this experience—we would add that we do *not* see ourselves as better than anyone. But *since* our receiving the fuller workings of the Holy Spirit—and to His credit—*we do testify of ourselves that we are better Christians than we each were before.*

A genuine work of the Holy Spirit at any dimension in a human soul will inevitably accomplish two things: (1) He will deepen our perspective on Christ's character and Christian purity, and (2) He will expand our freedom in worship and heighten our joy in living. The first work brings a progressive humility with a heightened awareness of sin and a greater readiness to confess and renounce it. The second is equally biblical, realizing the overflow of a promised facet of life in God's Kingdom: "For the Kingdom of God is not meat and drink, but righteousness, peace, and joy in the Holy Spirit" (Rom. 14:17).

The truly Spirit-filled experience will more than likely align with Christ's: "Then Jesus was led up by the Spirit into the wilderness to be tempted by the devil" (Matt. 4:1). Spirit-fullness is a pathway to a more direct conflict with our adversary than before. That's not a fatalistic proposition, as though the spiritual "upper" of a release in Spirit-filled language was a guarantee of an immediate "downer" through facing spiritual conflict. But a person who chooses to move into the Spirit-filled exercise of spiritual language will still face temptation, and because no badge of infallibility will instantly appear on his vest, *more* dependence on the Lord—not less—will characterize him. The realm of spiritual vitality is the realm of spiritual warfare. They're the same arena. And any notion of infallibility needs to be dashed to the ground because it's the surest way to fail: "Therefore let him who thinks he stands take heed lest he fall" (1 Cor. 10:12).

Perhaps the greatest battle of my entire personal spiritual life took place at a time I had made my deepest commitment to move in the realm of Holy-Spirit-fullness of power and pursuit. It was early in my ministry and without the least quest on my part for "an affair," I slowly but definitely began to find myself in an emotional entrapment. My marriage was strong and my commitment to Christ and Christian purity was solid. But my regular involvement with a woman of equal dedication evolved into an affinity which in time moved from friendship to a near-adulterous infatuation.

During those dark days of a temptation to which I never surrendered, I wrestled long in prayer against the emotional tentacles seeking to tangle my soul and drag me into sin. Alone at home, I would often cry out to God—frequently with surges of the spiritual language gushing forth in intercession for my own helplessness. It is to the praise of God's grace and the almightiness of His mercy that I was spared the loss of my integrity, my marriage, my ministry—my life!

There is no way I can ever measure the place of the spiritual language in "offloading" my burden, or in penetrating to the core of my need. But I *do* know two things: (1) that Spirit-fullness is no guarantee of infallibility; and (2) that the spiritual language is a mighty resource when in warfare against sin—whether in general, or in reference to one's own struggle. Though I speak with tongues, I am not rendered less than a fallible person. And,

• Though I speak with tongues, *I am a growing person*. To acknowledge oneself as "growing" is synonymous with acknowledging the need that every believer continue to do so. It is possible that nothing more thwarts Christian growth than the pretentiousness of any pattern of *posturing*, of supposed "attainment," however piously manifest. Such a "static" state of imagined accomplishment preempts the dynamic growth the Lord intends for us. Jesus described our relationship with Him as vine-to-branch, and in doing so not only promised growth but demanded fruitfulness. The religiousness He encountered in ancient Jerusalem was the embodiment of the nothing-but-leaves fig tree He cursed outside the city. His feelings about fruitlessness are clear, and it's the reason I need to keep keenly available to His primary method of assuring growth and fruit: *pruning*.

I propose that every Holy-Spirit-filled believer welcome the ceaseless ministry of our Lord in this respect. Nothing is truer of our religious traditions than their readiness to become excess baggage rather than fruit-begetting habits. The test of my growth will ultimately be measured by the regularity of my having been pruned—the flesh cut back, my "holy habits" scrutinized under God's fiery gaze, my "convictions" subjected to His modifying mercifulness, and my "doctrines" kept shapable by the Holy Spirit's increasingly growing me in my understanding of the Father and His Word.

It was early in my teenage years of exposure to the message of Holy-Spirit-fullness that one night I heard Esther Kerr Rusthoi speak. This frail-but-mighty woman, who composed one of this century's tenderest songs, "The Lover of My Soul," had selected Philippians 3:13–14 as a text for her teaching. Her ministry was used not only to rivet Paul's words into my soul, but to fix them in my heart as my "life text":

> Brethren, I do not count myself to have apprehended; but one thing I do, forgetting those things which are behind and reaching forward to those things which are ahead, I press toward the goal for the prize of the upward call of God in Christ Jesus.

A growing person will never become a bigot, for he or she knows there is much to learn; nor can a growing person ever be satisfied with the status quo, for the "onward call" continually sounds from the plateau above where our Great Shepherd stands and calls us to higher ground.

> I'm pressing on the upward way, new heights I'm
> gaining every day,
> Still praying as I onward bound, Lord plant my feet on
> higher ground!
>
> Johnson Oatman, Jr.

Though I speak with tongues, I realize I have not "arrived" at anything—for I am not rendered less than a growing person. And,

• Though I speak with tongues, *I am a dependable person.* There is a mild heresy among a few supposed charismatics, that to be alive in Holy-Spirit-fullness is to license a basic unpredictability to every facet in life. They are hard to pin down, and their argument will sometimes stem from the text in Acts 8 where Philip the Evangelist is suddenly wafted away by the Holy Spirit to another city—apparently transported miraculously (Acts 8:39–40). The idea of such who-knows-where-I'll-be-next-ism is interpreted as being purportedly "tuned in to God," or "in the flow of the Spirit." But instead, it in actuality becomes an attempt at spiritualizing irresponsibility or undependability. Thereby a person can explain *any* late arrival, *any* unpaid bill, *any* neglected duty, or *any* overlooked obligation—socially, financially, domestically, professionally—with the words, "Well, the Holy Spirit seemed to lead me to . . . ," or, "Sorry, but it must have been God's will, because I was . . ."

Of course, this runs absolutely crosscurrent to the true flowing of the Holy Spirit. The river of *life* will never spew out the sloppiness or the bitterness that is begotten by such shenanigans. Try to dress up undependability in the supposedly spiritual garments of respectability and you'll find this designer label garb is fabricated in mixed-up minds at best or in hell at worst.

The whole of the Scriptures breathe of a consistency between spirituality and dependability. Of course, life does contain unpredictables, and generous souls will always be understanding toward those circumstances which occasion delay, postponement, alteration, or cancellation of plans. Late payments are not necessarily unchristian, nor are late arrivals, but the dependable person deals with such eventualities in a responsible way that doesn't blame God for the changes. Even when His providence is apparently at work, it's best to leave that interpretation to the person impacted by whatever change our circumstance introduces into theirs. It's neither your calling nor mine to shackle God with the blame for what is more likely something which has distilled from my own frailty, lack of foresight, or plain failure.

To function in the spiritual language *can* make a difference, however. There are many times when I am in prayer, simply opening a day or a subject with God in my private devotions, that I have covered the matter with *both*—praying "with the understanding" as well as "with the spirit" (1 Cor. 14:15). It is too frequent an occurrence to write off as coincidence. Time and again during such prayer times, reminders occur, clarification of plans or schedules come to mind, or practical guidance impresses itself on me, enabling my more effective fulfillment of relational expectations, vocational pursuits, or spiritual goals.

It was Joe Blinco, the beloved former associate of the Billy Graham Evangelistic Association, later executive director of Southern California's Forest Home Conference Center, who addressed this issue of Christian dependability so pointedly. I was one of a thousand pastors present when Joe drew our attention to Mark 6:3. "Isn't this man the carpenter, the son of Mary?" He commented:

> It's worthy of our attention to note that this passing reference to Jesus, with direct reference to His profession as a carpenter/contractor, contains the Greek definite article—He's called THE carpenter. The intent could so easily be overlooked, but let me cast it for you in words we can remember. The inquirers are saying something very direct, but within their remark is an indirect statement about Jesus as a part of the professional community. He was THE carpenter in Nazareth; as though one might say, "If you're looking for someone who'll do a reliable job, who is dependable as a worker, the carpenter you want in this town is a specific one—His name is Jesus, Joseph's son. If he quotes a price, he'll stick to it; if he says he'll be there at 8 A.M., he'll be on time; and if he promises a quality job, you can be sure you'll get it."[2]

Enough on this point, but it does crystallize the truth: though a person speaks with tongues by the Spirit of Jesus dwelling within them, there is no reason to expect him or her to be less than a dependable person. And,

• Though I speak with tongues, *I am a sinful person.* To acknowledge this is neither to build a case for future carnal intent nor to argue for a casual indifference toward ongoing sinfulness in one's life. It's simply to state what should be obvious: *no* spiritual experience renders any of us above the touch of sin or beyond its reach.

The Holy Spirit has been given to make us *holy*—it's His first name! But His sanctifying presence, as powerful as it may be to assist me in resisting sin's efforts at invading or pervading my life and habit, is only as purifying as my will is to let Him have full sway. In writing a group of people he addresses as Spirit-filled (Gal. 3:2), the apostle Paul still points the way to ensure a walk of holiness in contrast to carnal indulgence:

> I say then: Walk in the Spirit, and you shall not fulfill the lust of the flesh. For the flesh lusts against the Spirit, and the Spirit against the flesh; and these are contrary to one another, so that you do not do the things you wish.
>
> Galatians 5:16–17

Listen to the words: "the things you wish"! What an indictment of our fundamental bent to sinning *however* Spirit-filled we may have become. One of the most honest and candid acknowledgments of this fact about all of us was quoted to me by a friend who had been in conversation with David DuPlessis a few years before David's death. This giant of faith, who showed such leadership and humble fidelity to his mission as a bearer of the message of the Spirit-filled life to virtually every denomination and on every continent, was asked a very pointed question by a young man.

"Dr. DuPlessis, as a young Christian I'm committed to serving Jesus Christ with my whole heart and to living in purity—body, soul, and mind. Still, I sometimes have struggles with my thought life. Could you tell me, sir, about how old I'll be when improper thoughts—especially about women—won't tempt my mind any longer?"

Dear David, whose purity of life and fidelity to the truth was legendary, looked squarely into the eyes of the young man, and there, in the eightieth year of his life, said, "Son, when I get that old I'll let you know!"

There's something about the honesty in that response that commends the greatness of a leader who felt no constraint to pretend a piety which might have been automatically presumed of him. We aren't hearing a man who was being dragged down by temptation, but one who frankly acknowledged its continuing presence throughout all our lifetimes. The flesh never ceases being exactly that until the day our flesh will be shed like a veil and our spirits join our Maker for eternity. Only in heaven, and ultimately in our resurrected bodies, will there be no potential "handle" for sin to manipulate us. Until then, "walking in the Spirit" is the power pathway to purity, and it is certain that a daily walk of ceaseless prayer in the Spirit can only contribute to that sin-mastering way of life. Though I speak with tongues, I am not rendered other than a potentially sinful person; yet still, I'm one who—for all this lifetime—holds the hope of overcoming through the Holy Spirit's presence and power. And,

• Though I speak with tongues, *I am a biblical and Christ-centered person.* So much has gone before in this book that I doubt there is any reader who would doubt this statement. But I include it because central to this list of traits is this dual, foundational value: *The Word* and *The Lord!* Perhaps I ought to title this point, "Though I speak with tongues I am a sensitive, *woundable* person." Because the focus I am seeking to register here on the charismatic Christian's commitment to Christ and the Scriptures, seems to be assailed with sufficient frequency that I feel a peculiar defensiveness.

It is a bizarre fact that notwithstanding the objective, statistical evidence that:

1. Charismatic/pentecostal ministries total more converts than any other sector of Christianity today; that

2. The number of Charismatic/Pentecostal missionaries total far more than half of all Protestants today; and that

3. The central message of this group is "Jesus Christ and Him crucified," and the sole authority for their proclamation is the eternal Word of the Bible—the Holy Scriptures;

still, carping critics suggest a lack of conviction regarding either or both of these priorities.

Please forgive this digression, for it can seem self-congratulatory and that is farthest from my motives. Any fruit God has given or continues to pour forth to His glory among us who welcome the Spirit's gifts and power in full measure today is the product of His hand *alone!* If we say anything of ourselves, it is in the words of the wisdom Jesus taught us: "We are unprofitable servants for we have only done what it was our duty to do" (Luke 17:10). But this issue is more than simply noting fruit in the record of current church history in the making. There are very real *personal* points of Christ-and-the-Bible centeredness.

I've rarely met a person who entered the realm of exercising spiritual language but that either or both these matters are soon brought up, usually in words like these: "Since I opened to this dimension of the Holy Spirit's work in my life, Jesus has become so much more precious to me; worshiping God has become so much more vital." Or, "I don't know how to explain it, but since I received my spiritual language, the Bible has opened up with a new clarity and depth to my understanding. I can't get enough of it—I *love* the Word of God."

Exactly *how* speaking with other tongues enhances the matter of understanding the Scriptures or loving Jesus Christ is probably a matter of speculation. But it is clear that *both* the Bible and God's Son are central to the Holy Spirit's present program. He *breathed* the Bible into existence, and He *glorifies* Christ at every opportunity. So it's not surprising that though I speak with tongues, I am a Bible-centered, Christ-centered person. And,

• Though I speak with tongues, *I am a happy person.* It may be that among the most unsettling things which observers of charismatic people comment on is their exuberance, expressiveness, and joyfulness. As strange as it may seem, many Christians find it suggestive of something less than sufficiently reverent if a person becomes genuinely happy about God, or worship, or church services—as though to be so is to reduce the meaningfulness of these matters. There is more than a faint hint by many that such excitement can only be present if people are shallow. They intimate that the reason for happy charismatics is that they haven't really captured the weightiness of true godliness, or that they don't adequately sense the greatness and grandeur of the Almighty God.

I must admit that I am cautious myself. It makes me uncomfortable when people clap too much or laugh too readily in church settings. As a pastor whose approach is *very* positive and *often* flavored with humor, I still am watchful against the intrusion of either a silly or giddy attitude rising among those I lead.

Nonetheless, it's a peculiar thing that Christians often feel suspicious of just plain happiness—indeed, of *fun* in the classic sense. The derivation of the word "fun" is from the medieval English *fonne,* which referred to the foolish or the silly, and in that respect I would suggest that "fun" is inappropriate for a Christian on any terms! However, more classically, "fun" describes that which is lively, or which brings enjoyment or pleasure. And the point is not to focus on fun in the gatherings of God's people, but to raise the question as to whether there ought not be an element of this order of "happy" when the Father's family is together.

I remember hearing John Van Der Hoeven, former warden of the Garden Tomb in Jerusalem (a traditional site of Jesus' death and resurrection) as he described the response of a hippie who heard John's proclamation of what the site commemorates. The preacher had just declared the fullness of the forgiveness of sin, pointing to Golgotha's skull-like escarpment just east of the Garden, then indicating the Empty Tomb from which Jesus had risen and lives forevermore. The vagabond youth, who was circling the earth in search of reality, listened spellbound. Then, as John concluded, the boy called out from the crowd: "Mister, if what you say is true, there should be singing and dancing for joy at this site every day of the year!"

Who can say less than a hearty "Amen!"? In fact, who wouldn't want to shout "Hallelujah!"?

The triumphant joy so frequently witnessed among most charismatics is not usually due to a reckless or shallow mind-set, though there are times such unfocused giddiness has been observed. But most of the time, if there is joy, happiness, or exuberance's expressiveness, it's because a liberated view of propriety has gripped the worshipers. Like the hippie, whose candor expressed what few could disagree with, I have to admit that I have difficulty repressing just plain "happy" when I think about the abundance of grace which God's salvation has lavished upon us.

Of course there are times for deeply sobered moments as well, and no thinking person would deny the wisdom of making occasion for pensive, meditative, reflective worship with either silence or reserve. But silence is not a synonym for reverence, just as I am not proposing happiness as an equivalent of holiness. But both silence and happiness—reverence and joyfulness—deserve a place in our gatherings and in our lifestyle as believers. People who have lost their laughter have usually begun to take themselves too seriously and God's grace not seriously enough. Though I speak with tongues I have not become a pretentious mystic nor a religious, stodgy cleric. A human happiness with a holy sensitivity is happily included on my agenda. I haven't reduced the weightiness of the wonder of God to either the shallow or superficial. But I do allow for merriment in the spirit of the proverb which attests to the therapeutic power of such happiness:

> A merry heart does good, like medicine, but a broken
> spirit dries the bones.
>
> Proverbs 17:22

And further,

• Though I speak with tongues, *I am an average person.* Salvation was never intended to breed a race of supersaints! Yet it has unfortunately *not* been uncommon for a few charismatic people to fall prey to the notion that "supernatural" means something other than "human." There is a generally unspoken but nonetheless present myth that, "If you get all God has for you, you'll become a member of a super-race of Christians whose mission is to move throughout the planet like extraterrestrials, stunning mankind with your accomplishments."

Of course there are reasons for expecting the supernatural as a natural part of a believing life. Jesus *did* say, "The works that I do shall you do and greater than these shall you do." Jesus *did* say, "These signs shall follow those who believe, in my Name they shall lay hands on the sick and they shall recover." Jesus *did* say, "Heal the sick, raise the dead, cast out devils." There is no arguing with the Scriptures unless one is committed to theologizing interpretive schemes that preempt the miraculous today. We *are* appointed to not only welcome, but to *anticipate* supernatural things happening when we pray or minister in Jesus' Name! But such expectations have never been propagated in the Word as requiring anything more than people who are (1) newborn in Christ and (2) Spirit-filled by His hand. They need not become a superrace.

Redemption and spiritual enablement haven't been designed to make us *super*human but to make us *truly* human—the kind of human which mankind was originally intended to be at Creation. To miss this point will not only give rise to an almost humorous effort of some to *act* supernatural, but this sad order of miming usually results in breeding "characters," people who end up acting something *less* than human rather than as someone "more than."

Notice I've said that, as a charismatic, I'm an average *person*, not an average *sinner*. The reason is that "sinners," by reason of the fall of mankind, have already had God's originally intended order of life for humanity reduced to a sadly inherited level of mediocrity. That isn't to speak unkindly of any of us who are sinners to the core, for even in fallen humanity there are multiplied beauties, gifts, and glories still residing. But the problem is threefold: (1) *none* of these qualities can save a soul, (2) *most* of them are nurtured in carnal pride, and (3) *all* of them are less than they can become if resubmitted to their Maker and redeemed through Christ unto God's glory.

By "average person" I am referring to the enriching qualities that God has ordained to be shared in common by all His redeemed children. These are touched with magnificence at an eternal level while still being restricted to the transience of our temporal level of life. The redeemed, Spirit-filled Christian is a marvelous dichotomy, a paradox in motion, where both the finite and the infinite meet. Born again into the life of God's eternal Kingdom, miracles are within reach. But still living out our season of years "a little lower than the angels," we are creatures of mixed triumph and trial.

It's a thrilling thing to "taste of the powers of the world to come" (Heb. 6:5), for the incredibly mighty power of the living God courses through us at times, with waves of Holy Spirit power that are a present-moment foretaste of the eternity yet before us. These momentary invasions of our ordinariness make for wonderfully extraordinary possibilities, and flashes of glory often distill in real miracles in the here and now. Yet, we also often find ourselves groaning amid present sufferings, longing for the moment at Christ's coming when "this mortal shall put on immortality and this corruptible shall put on incorruption" (Rom. 8:22–23; 1 Cor. 15:51–53). To live in this holy tension between two worlds requires a rare balance, always contending for God's supernatural grace to find a conduit through our frail vessel, while at the same time refusing to deny our fundamental humanity or to dabble in the vanity of self-exalting pretentiousness. It takes divine grace and humility to let God's Spirit restore and empower us to be "average" in this way, in the middle of a world that is lost in its far-below-average order of life. •

Though I speak with tongues and have begun to experience the taste of the supernature thereby, it has not rendered me less than aware that such grace has not been given to exalt me to some low-level deity, but to reinstate God's intended order for my humanity. And,

• Though I speak with tongues, *I am a hope-filled, trusting person.* Defining "charismatic" is an impossible task in general terms. The breadth of the *communion* of Christians who share the expositional view of the Scriptures which sees the Holy Spirit's working as present; the scope of the *fellowship* which shares the experience of spiritual language and the beauty of its purposes; and the dimensions of difference among *denominations* and individuals who exercise active New Testament faith and realize its power—all these defy categories.

One common denominator is a conviction about the changelessness of Jesus Christ. "Jesus Christ is the same yesterday, today, and forever" (Heb. 13:8) is a biblical watchword which governs convictions. We hold that the Savior is as able, willing, and powerful today as He ever was, and He will minister presently the same way through His Body—His church—where people will allow Him to operate through them. This common denominator even dominates above the shared experience in spiritual language, for genuine charismatics are more interested in what they can allow Jesus Christ to do *through* them than they are for what He may do *for* them. Secure in the gift of eternal life, their focus is directed toward how they might spread that testimony in Jesus' Name and bear witness to His promise of eternal hope with confirming signs and wonders as God verifies His Word and glorifies His Son.

That's why people like me teach and talk a good deal about faith.

Whatever the need, wherever the pain, however hopeless the situation, whoever can be reached, touched, or helped—hope prompts prayer, rooted in the promises of God's unchanging Word.

However differently the exercise of the prayer of faith may be, the conviction abides with this band of Christians: Without God's power there's nothing we *can* do. Yet, unless we obey His call and pray in faith, there's nothing He *will* do! Jesus' own instruction that we pray, "Thy Kingdom come," is the timeless reminder that God's almighty rule of grace and power only enters where it's invited in this world. Faith exercised through humble yet bold and obedient prayer is the key, and it's been placed in our hands.

Thus, even though charismatics and pentecostals differ widely (and sometimes vociferously) on *how* faith works, the bottom line is that a person who prays with the Spirit is often directing that prayer toward impossible situations—convinced that "all things are possible to him who believes" (Mark 9:23). It is the conviction that the Holy Spirit is enabling intercession—that is, prayer that will address the prayer target more efficiently—that prompts such readiness to face the impossible in faith.

> Likewise the Spirit also helps in our weaknesses. For we do not know what we should pray for as we ought, but the Spirit Himself makes intercession for us with groanings which cannot be uttered. Now He who searches the hearts knows what the mind of the Spirit is, because He makes intercession for the saints according to the will of God. And we know that all things work together for good to those who love God, to those who are the called according to His purpose.
>
> Romans 8:26–28

The substance of those three verses present three great truths:

1. We all regularly face "things" we don't know how to pray about (v. 26).

2. The Holy Spirit will dramatically assist in prayer at such times (v. 27).

3. By this means, God's purpose and power are introduced into the situation (v. 28).

Conclusion: Things that otherwise *wouldn't* have "worked together for good," **do now,** because Holy-Spirit-inspired intercessory prayer has intervened. A different result has become realizable than would have been the case if the circumstance were merely surrendered to the course of this world, to human wisdom, to theologized passivity or to hell's workings.

No sensible Christian, however convinced in the power of faith, is arrogant enough to claim to have "mastered" faith. There is no one who has a magic key or perfect insight, and thus the fruit of our faith-filled prayers is not always what the human mind would dictate. And that's when the *highest* level of faith takes over—the faith that trusts God's faithfulness even when it appears that our prayers haven't won the day (at least not as *we* would have defined "victory").

Perhaps others would prefer an easier course:

- Resign everything to God's hands. Claim nothing in prayer except a passive, "Thy will be done." (But this prayer has overlooked the first part of the directive: "Pray, 'Thy Kingdom *come*'"; a summons that expects the entry of power more than simply resigning to the inevitable.)

- Avoid asking God to heal, or urging people to expect the unusual, for then you'll never be embarrassed. And then you can plead fidelity for *not* having "put God on the spot" in the eyes of those whose hopes you raise. (But this stance overlooks that God has *called* us to appeal to Him: "Ask of me and I will show you great and mighty things which you know not!" [Jer. 33:3].)

There are no formula answers, nor are there any guaranteed results. But the record *is* very clear on one thing: A great many prayers for unusual or miraculous manifestations of God's power *are* answered! They are far too many to be written off as "emotionally invoked," or "coincidental," or "the law of averages in recovery."

As an infant I was the victim of a birth defect which the physician told my parents would have taken my life before I was two years old. But a prayer request was sent to a church near where my parents lived. The request, submitted by my mother's cousin (neither were yet born-again Christians), was not told to my parents until *after* I had been pronounced healed, and that by the doctor who said his therapy had nothing to do with my physical restoration!

Further, as a three-year-old child, I was stricken with polio; a diagnosis my parents received from the doctor to which they'd taken me. My folks had now become believers in Christ and called for the elders of the church to pray for me. No one demeaned the doctor's counsel, no one mocked the medical community, no one decried the use of medicine. But my parents were simply at a point that man had done the best he could do, and it wasn't enough. I was healed, again as the result of "the prayer of faith."

In each of those cases, as with multiplied millions like them, a certain part of most prayers of that order involved praying *both* with the spirit and with the understanding. Can you see, dear reader, why I perceive a special beauty in spiritual language? There has been a good deal of it offered over my need, as when years ago those simple Christians simply prayed and watched God's wonderful grace as it was manifest in my healing! Though I speak with tongues, I *don't* always witness the miraculous or see the result I might have preferred, but I am a hope-filled and trusting person nonetheless. My hopes are founded in Christ and rooted in God's Word of promise, and my trust is unshaken when answers seem unseen, for abiding faith assures me that my Father's unchanging wisdom, love, and mercy is in operation—even when I don't *see* it.

> Now faith is the substance of things hoped for, the evidence of things not seen.
>
> Hebrews 11:1

Do these ten thoughts find resonance with you?

With them I've sought to diffuse certain presuppositions about people who speak with tongues—about charismatics or pentecostals. I'm sure that some who accept that designation wouldn't accept every word of my definition or explanations. But the vast majority *are* characterized by what I've written.

To open to the beauty of spiritual language does not destine you to become a wild-eyed fanatic, a rigid proponent of faith, a person preoccupied with health or wealth, or a giddy, excitable runner from one televised service to another. Charismatic *isn't* a stereotyped lifestyle managed by a pop theology or a manipulative leader. It's a biblical, Christ-centered, sensible, hope-filled, happy, trusting application of God's promises for today. It's a dimension of Christian living which is potential to people who sin, fail, and suffer, but who seek

God's holiness, depend on His grace, and believe for His presence and power in the middle of their tough times.

And when this life-in-the-Spirit lifestyle is committed to, grown in, and intelligently responded to, you can count on it—

You'll become more Christ-like than ever before,
    more dependable than you've ever been,
        and as one of God's "average" redeemed ones, find
            yourself endued with the Holy Spirit to *raise* the average of
                life. "Christ in you" becomes "the hope of glory," even in
                    a world that has fallen far below God's wondrous
                        design for mankind—His most beloved creature.

5

The Light Coming from Above

> Oh, the depth of the riches both of the wisdom and knowledge of God! How unsearchable are His judgments and His ways past finding out.
>
> Romans 11:33

Are the tongues that are exercised in the use of spiritual language actual languages or simply muddied speech—gibberish, as mockers take such delight in calling it?

The answer to that question ought to be addressed more humbly than is often the case, especially in light of the fact that no one could possibly make an analysis on the basis of his or her own experience. With approximately six thousand languages spoken on this planet, it's been posited by linguistic experts that there is no individual person who has ever gained a basic grasp of even as many as a hundred languages. Who with academic integrity could claim to assert that the language they heard a worshiper speak "was not a language at all," seeing the most trained observer would still have far more than five thousand languages he had no knowledge of—any one of which he may be hearing spoken by the tongue speaker?

Some Bible commentators have argued that the tongues of Pentecost are not only to be understood as a once-only-phenomenon, but that they were different from today's testimonies of spiritual language because they were recognized by those present from other nations. But look at the text:

> And when this sound occurred, the multitude came together, and were confused, because everyone heard them speak in his own language. Then they were all amazed and marveled, saying to one another, "Look, are not all these who speak Galileans? And how is it that we hear, each in our own languages in which we were

born? Parthians and Medes and Elamites, those dwelling in Mesopotamia, Judea and Cappadocia, Pontus and Asia, Phrygia and Pamphylia, Egypt and the parts of Libya adjoining Cyrene, visitors from Rome, both Jews and proselytes, Cretans and Arabs—we hear them speaking in our own tongues the wonderful works of God."

Acts 2:6–11

Having read that, nonprejudiced reading would seem to argue for the likelihood that, while there *were some* languages recognized, there probably were many more spoken than were identified.

We know from Acts 1:15 that there were 120 present at the visitation of the Holy Spirit in chapter 2. But in Acts 2:9–11 not even 20 different geographical regions are mentioned. Even if every hearer heard two or three worshipers speaking the language or languages he identified, there are still many more that may have been being spoken. It is doubtful that any individual present could even have known all the languages mentioned, so the report in the biblical narrative was doubtless summarized from the combined observations of several different hearers; people who said, "We hear them speaking in our own tongues the wonderful works of God."

I wish to submit that the languages spoken by people today who employ spiritual language under the enabling power of the Holy Spirit are all actual languages. I'm aware that a few instances of linguistic analysis conducted by experts who have scrutinized tapes of speakers in tongues have made such judgments as "gibberish," or "This does not contain the usual structures of recognizable speech." But my own experience and that of many other pentecostals and charismatics I have met strongly argue against this laboratorial judgment.

Furthermore, Paul's words in 1 Corinthians 13 specifically mention the possibility that the early church viewed some of their languages spoken in prayerful worship as "tongues . . . of angels." I hasten to say that I am not asserting this proposition—*the Bible does.* It is not *my* argument that some tongues spoken by the Holy Spirit's power may be only understood in heaven, it is *Paul's* intimation that suggests it. And it is doubtless the apostle's humility before that fact that caused him, even in a setting where he was dealing correctively, to affirm:

There are, it may be, so many kinds of languages in the world, and none of them is without significance. Therefore, if I do not know the meaning of the language, I shall be a foreigner to him who speaks, and he who speaks will be a foreigner to me.

1 Corinthians 14:10–11

For so many years the old Authorized Version of the Bible used the words "*unknown* tongues" in 1 Corinthians 14. Even though the italicized form of the word "unknown" was intended to indicate the translators had supplied a word not included in the original Greek text, the terminology was constantly bandied about. Even pentecostals referred to their speaking with tongues as being "unknown tongues." This "unknown," of course, has *always* been true to the understanding of the speaker, but not necessarily true of the language being spoken. Because I find, or anyone else hearing me finds, the spiritual language I am speaking "unknown" to him or her in no way categorizes the tongue as verifiably "unknown" throughout the earth (or the heavens, for that matter!).

Supporting this conviction is a small body of evidence from my own experience; experience which I claim as not confined to my experience as though I were a favored party. While such episodes as follow may not be widely proliferated, they are frequent enough that honest inquirers into the nature and value of spiritual language will find assurance that this linguistic miracle is not meaningless utterance or gibberish.

Speak to Him in Tongues

It is unquestionably one of the most disarming and remarkable experiences of my life as a Christian!

The day began like so many on my personal calendar—getting onto an airplane to go speak somewhere. But this day I was on my way home, having ministered the night before in Portland, Oregon. I stepped aboard the plane, looking forward to the relaxation of a restful two hours over breakfast and of gazing at some of the most beautiful peaks anywhere on earth—the snow-capped cones which help form the evergreen spine of the Cascades.

I had hardly seated myself in the first-class cabin when a well-dressed man in a business suit slid his briefcase into the overhead compartment and took his seat beside me. Even though I had anticipated privacy and a time for prayerful meditation while flying above such natural splendor as lay ahead, I greeted the man (let's call him Bill) and a casual conversation began.

We had exchanged pleasantries—the usual, "Out on business or on your way home?" inquiry, and I found that this was but one leg of several stops for him.

The plane lifted off and for a few minutes I enjoyed the spectacle of Mount Hood, glistening in the morning sunlight to the east of the Rose City—Portland—which lay below straddling the Willamette River and bordering the mighty Columbia. My heart swelled with praise to God for the excellence of His artistry!

The flight attendant had just set our trays into place, and a delicious breakfast was before me (I'm *not* an "airline food" critic, and fortunately so, as much as I travel; I *like* it!) I had turned my head to study the loveliness below again and at the same time offered thanks for my food—choosing not to "bow" over my meal, not by reasons of shame but to avoid appearing pretentious. As I opened the linen napkin and spread it on my lap, an exchange between Bill and me reopened the conversation as we ate.

It was earlier, when we had introduced ourselves, that I had detected a Southwestern accent to his voice and asked if he were from the South. His response was not quite embarrassed, but he was slightly apologetic. I hastened to assure him my observation was positive, that I enjoyed all flavors of Southern drawls, to which he responded:

"You know, it's a funny thing, but I guess I've always been inclined to feel awkward about my speech. I didn't mean to seem defensive, but it goes back to the fact that I didn't really begin speaking English until I was almost five years old."

He explained further, "I was raised in Oklahoma, and my mother was a full-blooded Indian of the Kiowa tribe. When I started to school, I was still limited in my English, and I think I still feel a kind of hangover embarrassment going back to when the kids used to mock me in school."

That's when it happened.

The instant he spoke those words, another set of words whispered within my heart, *Speak to him in tongues.* It happened so quickly, and the prompting was so startling in its implications, I simply let the thought register in my mind but took no immediate action.

My mind was now operating on two tracks. On the one, I was continuing the conversation with Bill, but on the other, I was trying to assess the strange—nearly frightening—prompting I had received. I knew the Voice, and I understood what had been said. What I didn't know, however, was why in the world God would give me such an assignment, and how in the world I could fulfill it without seeming a total and complete idiot. The result was that I simply allowed our conversation to continue, without any effort on my part at steering it.

He was a civil engineer, and as we talked I discovered the diverse projects he had been involved in, and in some especially exotic locations. When he mentioned having recently completed a project in Israel, I responded by asking as to where in Israel, explaining that I had been in the Holy Land myself only a few months before.

"What were you doing in Israel?" he asked.

"I was leading a study tour of Middle Eastern Bible lands, and the majority of our time was spent in Israel. As a pastor and teacher I do this with some regularity, because Israel is such a treasure trove of information—both on ancient Bible history as well as on contemporary Bible prophecy."

When he looked interested at the mention of prophecy, I cited one or two recent events that had occurred in Israel and how they indicated the fulfillment of Scriptures linked to Jesus Christ. The Name of Jesus drew a visible twitch of Bill's mouth, and he responded.

"I've never been much of a believer of things regarding Christ or the Bible. Church has generally seemed irrelevant, and whenever I've tried to read the Bible it seemed too out of date."

"I know what you mean, Bill," I agreed. "In fact, one of the reasons I think the church I lead has grown so much is that we have confronted that problem. There is a growing number of congregations like ours today—places where the worship is alive and contemporary, and where the Bible is not only made practical but newer translations are used." He nodded acceptingly, but nonetheless registered his skepticism.

"I have no criticism to make of people who believe in God, but I find faith something that seems improbable to me. My scientific studies have made me very doubtful about such matters."

Again, I responded with agreeableness. "I know what you mean; in fact, contrary to what many people think about pastors and Bible teachers, we have our own bouts with unbelief and skepticism too." He looked mildly surprised.

"Perhaps one of the best things that's ever happened to me," I continued, "was the discovery of the large body of literature that has accumulated over the centuries—books written by Christian scholars who have faced the tough questions which bring doubts to people like you and me. For example, Bill, have you ever heard of C. S. Lewis?"

I was surprised that he hadn't, since Lewis's works have been so widely disseminated in both the Christian as well as the secular academic community, but I didn't indicate my surprise—I simply moved ahead.

"Lewis was a professor at both Oxford and Cambridge universities in England, who, having been an atheist, came to admit that honesty with history and confronting clear reasoning brought him to faith in Jesus Christ. Though he was an acknowledged Christian, no one ever suggested it dulled his academic brilliance or intellectual respectability. His lectures at Cambridge were regularly packed out, even though his field of specialty was medieval literature. And a further testimony to his intellect is that the Encyclopedia Britannica Corporation added his book, *The Abolition of Man* to their Great Books of the Western World series within less than a decade of his death in 1963."

My seat partner was showing definite interest as I explained Lewis's accomplishments, which led me to the point. "All this, Bill, is just to give background on a book I think *any* reader would profit from, Christian or not. Its title is *Mere Christianity,* and it's essentially written for people who have difficulty with faith or find little reason to believe in God."

I paused, then added: "And as for reading the Bible in outdated language, one of the most widely distributed books today is *The Living Bible,* which is simply the Bible in a modern, highly readable, contemporary idiom."

I wasn't trying the patience of my listener. He was clearly interested and was hearing and weighing my words. I concluded: "I've found these two books so helpful to my own thought and questions, I've shared them both with many people. I don't want to obligate you or seem pushy in making the offer, but if you would like I'd be glad to make a gift of these two small volumes and mail them—*Mere Christianity* and the New Testament in *The Living Bible.*"

Bill set his coffee cup down, thoughtfully considering my offer for a moment, then said, "That's very kind of you, Jack, but frankly, I don't think I'd read them. Like I said, I'm really not much of a believer."

I smiled and expressed my understanding of his position, and I turned the conversation to other things which kept the moment from becoming awkward for him. After a little while, our breakfast concluded, we both turned to reading we had brought with us. But I had a problem.

That Voice. The Lord, prompting me by His Holy Spirit, had given me a directive almost an hour before that had been so clear. And it had also been terribly demanding; that is, not in its tone or insistence, but in the action it called for—*Speak to him in tongues.*

Right now, I want to make one thing clear to anyone reading my account. The first is, I didn't like the idea. Don't anyone think this was something I was about to do, or that I was so enamored with spiritual language I was looking for situations where I could blurt it out publicly. If anything would have been farther from my mind, it would have been on the order of leaping to the aisle and doing a fan dance, or possibly suggesting to Bill we both step outside and fly alongside the jet!

But one thing I've learned is not to talk back to God, at least not so He can hear me!

I mused over the prompting I'd received, wanting to stand erect before the Almighty and shout, "Speak to him in tongues? Sure! That's easy for *You* to say, but what about me sitting here at thirty-five thousand feet ending up looking like a religious kook!" But I didn't protest; I quietly inquired of my own mind how God might expect me to deliver this message. It was a ticklish proposition to say the least.

About thirty minutes later, Bill laid down the book he'd been reading, and since it seemed natural to resume conversation, I took a course of action which I felt God's wisdom was showing me.

"You know, I was thinking a few minutes ago about your comment when we first sat down and I asked about your Southern accent. It's so interesting to me that you would, in fact, know another language and still feel even remotely embarrassed. Most of us Americans only know one, and *that* embarrasses me often when I travel to other countries."

"Like I said," he laughed, "I guess I feel that because of the things kids do to kids when they're little."

"Bill," I said, "I've been sitting here with the most curious thought. I wonder . . ." I hesitated. "I wonder—you know, quite a long time ago I was 'taught' some words in a language I don't know. And thinking about your familiarity with your native Kiowa Indian tongue, just out of curiosity—as I said, I wondered if you would mind if I said some of those words, just on the chance that you might recognize their meaning."

"Sure," he responded without the least hesitation. "Go ahead."

I looked away from his face, my eyes focused on the upholstery pattern on the back of the seat in front of him, and in a conversational tone began to speak in my spiritual language. I had hardly begun when it seemed I turned a linguistic corner, and I heard myself speaking a language unlike any I'd heard in prayer before. The total length of all I spoke was approximately the length of this paragraph. I stopped and looked back at Bill.

His response was immediate and businesslike. "That's a pre-Kiowan language, from which our Kiowa Indian tongue came." I remained amazingly composed, even though everything inside me wanted to shout, "IT IS?!—HALLELUJAH!") He continued: "I don't know all the words you spoke, but I do know the idea they express . . ." I could hardly believe what he was saying—I was overwhelmed, yet totally reserved in my outward demeanor.

"What are they about?" I asked.

"Well," he gestured in an upward fashion with his hand. "It's something about the light that's coming down from above."

It was a Holy Spirit setup, and I recognized what I was to say now.

"Thanks, Bill. That's amazing that this has happened. I really appreciate your letting me make that inquiry." He gestured simply, saying, "Not at all. It *is* interesting."

The crucial part faced me now, but what had happened was too incredible to attribute to anyone else than the Spirit of God. I had to finish what had been given me to do, and I did it this way.

"You know, Bill, I've got a confession to make. Do you mind?"

He looked puzzled at first, but seeing my smile, responded with a quizzical smile of his own. "Sure, whatever." I started to proceed, just as the pilot announced we were starting our descent and would be arriving at LAX in a matter of minutes. I sensed God's profoundly timing this encounter, as well as so unusually prompting its content.

"Have you ever heard or read of people who speak with tongues in worship or in prayer?"

He affirmed that he had, listening attentively without any apparent discomfort.

"Well, my confession is twofold—the first part being that that way of praying is a part of my own personal practice. The difficulty in admitting it to someone I hardly know is that one never knows if the person you tell this to might think the next thing you're going to do is pull out some snakes or start foaming at the mouth." His laughter joined mine, making clear that he was with me; that is, not unreceptive to what I was saying. "But the second part of my confession is more difficult; not because you've made me less than comfortable, but because I don't want to seem weird or peculiar to you.

"I don't know, Bill, what it sounds like to you if somebody says they felt God impressed them to do something, but I have to admit to you that when we first began talking this morning I sensed His voice to me." The man's attention was completely given to me. He wasn't showing anything of suspicion, but rather that my credibility as a sensible person had already been established earlier. He was listening.

"What I felt I was to do was impressed upon my mind at the moment you mentioned your being brought up with the Kiowan language as your mother tongue, so to speak. It was in that instant—I don't know how this will sound to you—but then, I sensed an inner voice saying to speak to you in the language I use in prayer at times.

"I didn't do this as a stunt—in fact, everything of my human reasoning would have preferred to not do it at all. But I felt that somehow I must obey that prompting. The significant thing to me, and which I think will interest you, is that right after I began to speak to you, the language I usually speak changed—and so remarkable to me is that you made any identification of it at all." I broke off for a moment to allow the presence of the moment to settle in, for there was a distinct sobriety on his face and an unusual sense of the Holy Spirit's anointing on my soul.

"Forgive me, Bill, because I don't want to be insensitive. Okay?"

"No," he nodded positively. "It's okay. . . . Go ahead."

"Well, I can't escape a sense of God's intending something very special for both of us today. I want you to know that I respect your skepticism and acknowledged doubts, just as I recognize you have been friendly toward me, knowing my Christian convictions. But when you interpreted what you understood of the language I spoke—and remember, it was different than is customary to me—I must admit it seems to me the Lord Himself, as the Light that is coming from above, is seeking to get your attention about how real He really is."

The jet aircraft was now on its glide path, only hundreds of feet above houses, streets, and parking lots—only seconds from touchdown. Bill was looking straight ahead as I had spoken the last words, and now he was silent; a businessman pensively evaluating a decision. He turned to me with warmth and matter-of-fact directness: "Jack, you know those two books you said you'd send me?" I motioned affirmatively. He reached into his pocket and took out a business card and, while beginning to jot his home address on it, continued, "I want to accept your offer. If you'll send them, I promise you—I will read them." I took his card, the plane wheeled into its gate, and within minutes we were parted.

There wasn't more to be done in that conversation; I knew that. I suppose every Christian hearing this story, including me, would prefer an ending with Bill's head bowed and my leading him to Christ. But that wasn't on the agenda that day, and though I sent Bill the books, I never heard from him. All I know is that God not only challenged my will to trust Him in an unforgettable way, but he also impressed His personal presence and truth upon a settled unbeliever in an unsettling way. It seemed an example of something in God's Word.

In both Jesus' words and Paul's, tongues are referred to as a sign, one which Paul specifically says may become convincing to an unbeliever (Mark 16:17; 1 Cor. 14:22). While I don't know what became of the seed of God's Word sown through the Bible and book sent to this scientist, I do know I saw a man's countenance and disposition toward the things of God completely reverse in the face of a sign-gift I was privileged to deliver.

To relate that story creates an unusual sense of vulnerability in me. As exposed to the possibility of misunderstanding as I felt I might be that day, it is only compounded multiple times over when writing or speaking it as I have and am. I can imagine questions: "What did it feel like to have such an unusual experience?" Answer: I didn't feel *anything* (other than stunned amazement when Bill recognized the essence of the words I spoke). I only felt a call to believe the prompting of the Holy Spirit and to do what I sensed was the will of God for that moment. Perhaps someone may ask, "Would you do that again?" Or, "What if he had recognized nothing of what you spoke, how would you have felt?" Answers: I *hope* I would obey if I was prompted to do that again, and if Bill had not recognized what I had said, I would simply have left the matter with the Lord. The way I expressed it to him, any nonidentification would have been an unawkward end to the matter. But for me, privately, it would have obviously prompted the question, "Was that really the Lord speaking to me?" Still, I think I know how I would have answered that eventuality. The Voice was so clear I couldn't doubt it, and I would have concluded God was simply testing my obedience to risk my pride and humble my soul. As it turned out, it became far more humbling than I could ever have imagined, for God did such an amazing thing—beyond what I would have expected and beyond what human reason could have done in cutting through the doubting mien of a God-doubting, skeptical materialist.

Even more remarkable to me are stories like this which have actually resulted in known cases of conversion.

Conversion Episodes

When I first met Evelyn Thompson in 1962 she and her husband were already legendary. Their ministry of evangelism in the Philippines, on the island of Mindanao, not only was attended by a flow of miracle works of God's grace and power in healing and delivering many, but the profundity of their church-planting success occasioned their being a centerpiece in Jim Montgomery's book, *New Testament Fire in the Philippines.*

Evelyn is a slight, almost frail, graying woman with a gracious, regal bearing about her. Though now well into her eighties, she still preaches frequently, not only having a refreshing ministry in God's Word, but also being uniquely possessed of a style that conveys spiritual authority without sacrificing a gentle femininity. This lady has probably experienced as many miracles through her ministry as anyone in this century, but the fact that they were ministered in the jungles of South Pacific islands, beyond the reach of the media and without fanfare, has kept her relatively unknown. Her ministry has been trusted and confirmed in her denomination since the 1930s when she served as a layperson in the Long Beach Foursquare Church, the same church my parents attended the night they received Christ. In the 1940s, Evelyn, with the strong assistance of her administratively gifted husband, founded a Christian school in San Diego County, and later they answered God's call to the foreign mission field.

In private conversation with them both (until Arthur's death a few years ago) I have heard story after story of the power of God's grace in evangelism. But none is more moving than the one that follows; a story I asked Evelyn to dictate so I would have the particulars correct from the lips of the person who experienced this miracle moment—one that was witnessed by several colaborers at the time.

Evelyn Thompson

While being a missionary in the southern parts of the Philippines on the island of Mindanao, where there are many jungles—interior places not usually reached by anyone, really. We were on a trek to reach a new village. It was from that area that a woman had come—a woman who was completely out of her mind. The villagers had not known what to do with her at all, and they brought her to a place near the ocean where, on the sand, a house on stilts had been built—high stilts, maybe twelve feet high. It was made of bamboo rounds and looked more like a cage than a place for a human being. My husband and I were brought up into that house with several other people to pray for this woman who was chained to the bamboo floor. It was very sturdy; she could not get loose.

As soon as we walked into that room, we realized what was happening, as the Holy Spirit made known to us the demonic nature of the problem with her. There was a small baby in the corner of the room lying on a mat. It was her baby—a beautiful baby—but she could not take care of it, and someone else was doing that. As we came in and almost immediately began to pray for her, the woman began to rant and rave. We prayed as one would usually pray in such a setting; we prayed with power, we prayed in the language of the Holy Spirit—but still nothing seemed to happen.

Finally, I said to the people, "Those of you who do not believe or cannot have the faith to release this woman from the chains that bind her soul, please leave the room." All but three left, and my husband, another man, and I were left. Then we prayed again. At first, when I laid hands on her, she calmed—but nothing happened. Great compassion filled my soul and I cried out, "Oh God, what can I do here? I cannot leave this place without Your doing something here that I can see, that this woman would be delivered!" I began to pray again with such passion that my husband put his arms around me, feeling concerned for the way I was pouring myself out in prayer. We still had much to do on this journey, and he was concerned for the ebbing of my strength in the tropical heat. But I asked him to release me and allow me to pray until I sensed victory, and he agreed.

I began to pray again, and as I did, out of my mouth—like a ball of fire from the middle of my stomach—came another language that I had never spoken before in the Spirit; certainly a language that I had never learned, nor had I ever heard it before. But as it came out of my mouth, I saw that there was a change in the expression on the face of the woman we were praying for. I saw that her eyes were listening, and at once I began to understand that I was speaking her language.

As this change came over her, I saw the muscles in her face begin to relax, the trembling stopped, and her hands ceased the wild beating of the air as though she were trying to hit me. She had been writhing almost like a slithering snake, and this, too, ceased as well as her constant laughing over her shoulder in a hysterical way. Then a most wonderful thing happened.

I not only could see that she understood *me,* but suddenly *I* was enabled to understand what I was saying; I was able to think as well as to speak in a language which I had never learned and never heard before! In the following minutes I explained the story of Jesus Christ, God's gift to us, and how Jesus had died for our sins and rose from the dead. And with a perfect awareness of every word I was speaking, I led her to the Lord Jesus Christ with full understanding of that language at that time.

She was totally delivered and today she still lives. She became a witness to the Resurrection power of the Lord Jesus Christ, was restored to her husband that very day, and took her baby and nursed it. Now, these many years later, she knows the Lord and has raised her children accordingly.

I did not know that language after that one instance. I later heard that language spoken by others in the mountain areas, but could not understand it and I certainly could not speak it.

How great is our God! How blessed to be filled with His Holy Spirit and to have faith that He knows His way when we don't. He *will* lead us and guide us.

Another case of evangelism being advanced by the sign-gift of tongues is related by Jamie Buckingham in his book, written during his struggle with cancer. Eighteen months before his body finally succumbed to the disease, an unusual period of divine grace attended the season he first experienced the onset of the affliction. In *Summer of Miracles,* Jamie describes an unexpected happening as he was at the hospital waiting for the technicians to scope his own body in search of the disease that had attacked this beloved man of God.

Jamie Buckingham

Waiting for them to set up the gamma ray scan in the room across the hall, I noticed a feeble-looking man lying on a gurney in the hall. I walked over to him. He was a mere shadow, just bones covered by jaundiced skin. One leg had been amputated, and he had tubes running out of his body into bottles suspended on poles above the stretcher. I looked into his emaciated face. He was Oriental—perhaps Korean. Totally uninhibited, I reached out my hand, placed it on his fragile shoulder and starting praying in the Spirit. Quietly.

"He can't understand you," a nurse said as she stepped out of a nearby doorway. "He speaks only Korean."

"It's OK," I winked. "I wasn't praying in English."

I looked down, and the old man was smiling, great tears flooding his eyes. With one bony hand he reached up and touched my arm. He nodded. He may not have spoken any English, but one thing was certain—he understood.

I squeezed his shoulder gently and went into the room where I was to have the next scan. The technician wanted me to stand against a drum-shaped piece of equipment that would take pictures of my hip and kidney area. I could see the vague shapes flashing on a large monitor across the room. When it was over and I started out of the room, I noticed an older woman sitting in a wheelchair just inside the door. Her head was drooping. She was in obvious pain.

"May I pray for you?" I was astounded at my boldness. Never in my life had I approached a total stranger and prayed for them. Yet within the last ten minutes I had done it twice.

She slowly raised her head. "Are you a priest?"

"No, just a follower of Jesus."

"Oh! Yes, please. I hurt so much."

I put my hand on her head and prayed softly. "Lord, in obedience to Your command to lay hands on the sick . . ."

"Oh!" She flinched under my hand. "What was that?"

"What was what?"

"I feel so much better."

I reached down and kissed her cheek then headed back toward the waiting room. Something—Someone—had taken control of my mind and body.[1]

Several pages later, after unfolding many of the events of God's dealings with his own soul through his struggle with disease, Jamie returns to tell the rest of the story about the Korean man for whom he had prayed in tongues in the hospital hallway. Now, it was the following Sunday, after church—

As we were leaving the building that morning I was stopped by Vince Anderson and his wife, Jung Hi, a Korean. She was weeping.

"That man, that Korean man you prayed for in the hospital . . . that is my Korean daddy. He is in a nursing home . . . he is dying . . . he did not know Jesus. Yesterday he told me in Korean he had accepted Jesus."

Her voice broke, and she threw her arms around me, holding tightly. "He now knows Jesus. He is ready to die. Thank You, thank You, God."

I held her as she wept. Looking up I saw Vince's handsome face. He too was weeping—his arms around both of us.

"Thank You, thank You, God!"[2]

Besides these accounts of tongues being a sign to an unbeliever in an evangelistic sense, within my experience there are other ways in which I have seen God sovereignly use my spiritual language to prompt faith in His supernatural grace for today.

I am always amazed to receive word of some new corner of our planet where audio cassette tapes of my teachings have arrived. With more than three thousand titles having been distributed, totaling somewhere between one and two million cassettes, unusual settings and thrilling testimonies abound.

One such testimony arrived from a Southern Baptist missionary in Thailand, who had formerly been schooled in the belief that speaking in tongues was not for today and that where they are heard, they are nothing more than gibberish. The letter was not written to focus on tongues but primarily to thank us for the ministry in the Word of God that was bringing strength and encouragement to this couple. As a virtual footnote, they mentioned in passing:

> Incidentally, on one of your recent tapes you brought a message in tongues at the end of the sermon, and then you interpreted it. We thought you might be interested to know that a part of the "tongue" was pure Thai, and the interpretation you brought was precisely what the Thai words meant.

An Unnecessary Struggle

The purpose of relating these perfectly clear incidents is not to suggest that they recommend special tribute to any of us who have experienced such confirmation of the reality of the spiritual language today. Nor should these be thought rare. Even though this order of manifestation may be sporadically experienced in the life of any individual (I've had four instances of languages I've spoken being recognized), there are sufficiently abounding testimonies to warrant that once for all the "gibberish" notion should be set aside.

I have often heard people speak with tongues, whose spiritual language sounded very undeveloped. But I have determined to leave that with them and the Holy Spirit, with the simplest counsel that they prayerfully expect their prayer language to expand and develop. To struggle with the question of the reality of true languages being spoken is as unnecessary as wrestling with the question of the contemporaneity of the spiritual language as a promised blessing for today's Christian. It may on occasion be a sign to an unbeliever as these cases testify, but in every case, where spiritual language is received and employed with regularity and practical wisdom, there are beautiful benefits attending this practice.

However, it is often the case that benefits awaiting in our spiritual journey cannot be welcomed or realized until obstacles are overcome. Let me describe a big one. One I had to face from one side of the wall and which may face you from the same viewpoint . . . or from the other.

6

Historic Landmarks—
Broadening Boundaries

While God ordained that the landmarks in ancient Israel be respected, He never ordered that those landmarks become the people's boundaries.

As a father, one of the most moving moments to touch my heart took place recently, when the elders of our congregation commissioned Anna's and my youngest son, Mark, and his wife, Deirdre, to missionary service. Now, with several years of pastoral experience to their record, they were entering a new season in their ministry as, with their three small children, they were answering a call to Norway; a call extended from Norwegian leaders who invited them to come and labor in church planting and teaching ministry there.

In his commissioning sermon, Mark related an incident that had long ago become an entrenched part of our Hayford family folklore: The Saga of the Red Line. The red line epic goes back to Mark's childhood, when he drifted from the house one morning, wandering down the street and around the corner; a straying three-year-old in slow pursuit of his older brother who had left for school. Jack, our oldest son, purposefully en route to school, was unaware of his brother's attempt to follow him, and no one in the house knew Mark had left. It not only was an occasion of high consternation for Anna and me when we made the discovery of his absence and the wild search began, but it was a memorable moment for Mark's "stern" too, after we found him! Though but three years old, he knew the boundaries and understood rules, and his punishment, while certainly not inappropriate for his age, was well understood too.

At first, our post-event fears tempted us to think we'd better put up a gate to protect against such an eventuality again, because we lived near downtown Los Angeles where a small boy could easily be at serious risk if he were loose on the streets. But we were a young family with little extra cash, and a gate seemed out of the question. So, since our kids were trained to respond to reasonable and explained guidelines, and since we believed Mark would heed a clear, visible reminder if we provided it at the point where the gate would have been installed, all I did was buy a can of bright red paint. I simply painted a red line across the driveway—a thin line, about one-half inch wide, which established a "landmark" as Mark's boundary line. It worked. And we never had any future problem.

But as Mark was preaching his farewell sermon, now a young thirty-year-old pastor about to step across international boundaries in following Christ's call, the red-line incident came into play again. While ministering that Sunday morning, he reached into the pulpit to bring out a broken piece of concrete—a jagged chunk of cement with a faded, barely visible red line on it. The sentiment of what followed touched everyone.

He explained how he had recently returned to the old homesite, happening by at the very time the building was being demolished for replacement with apartment units. Going over to the place where the driveway had been crushed, he had been happily surprised to find the piece of the original red line. With the object in hand, he explained how God had used this memento in His dealings with him and DeeDee, our daughter-in-law.

"This past year," Mark related, "I was at prayer one day and the Lord said, 'The red line isn't your boundary anymore.'" He continued by describing how God used a childhood incident to interpret the fact He was calling him beyond boundaries he presumed were lifelong—particularly the supposition his ministry would always be in the United States. He knew he was called "beyond his father's house" (that is, serving as he had the preceding three years on our pastoral staff). And the Holy Spirit had also spoken to him from Isaiah 54:2, "Enlarge the place of your tent, and let them stretch out the curtains of your habitations." It was these dealings which had prompted his return to our former house, and his timely discovery of the demolition underway.

I couldn't help but think of this homey story a few weeks later as I was talking with the leader of a major evangelical denomination. We were conversing about church renewal, and I was impressed by something he said. He's a discerning man, wisely perceptive of the challenge in his leadership role; one seeking to blend a sensitivity to his own church's history and traditions with the renewing summons he senses in today's call of the Spirit. In relating his burning sense of mission to lead his movement in the spirit of renewal which the Holy Spirit is spreading across the whole church throughout the whole world, he spoke a word of wisdom. He said to me, "I have determined to respect our ancient landmarks, but not to let them become our boundaries." This insightful guideline, which is derived from Solomon's counsel, "Remove not the ancient landmarks which your fathers have set" (Prov. 22:28), expresses something of a dilemma I faced a few years ago.

When renewal first came to our church, I felt I was walking a tightrope. I wanted to be sensitive to two things—both of which I felt were of equal importance. First, God was pouring "new wine" into our midst. The old wineskins of our church's traditions were being stretched with such blessing, yet we still didn't want an "explosion." How could I lead in a way that respected the Holy Spirit's earlier workings there and still be receptive to His present works? Maybe you've felt the same at a personal level.

Many of us are facing the Spirit's summons to "new wine." Like the leader I quoted, we all can hear His call. We sense the breezes of refreshing being breathed today by the Holy Spirit. But thoughtful people—most all of us—want to be unpresumptuous, to refuse the destructiveness of an iconoclastic or rebellious mind-set. Like my son Mark, the memory of boundaries marked out by the fathers of our earlier experience, creates an inner reserve to new things in Christ, until . . . until we listen to *the* Father's new call today.

It's a delicate challenge to answer a call to broadened boundaries when your life has been limited to specific landmarks. But it is possible to do so and to still retain a gentle spirit, to "enlarge the place of your tent" without despising or removing the respected monuments of tradition. I believe that in the Spirit of Jesus you and I *can* open ourselves to fresh dealings of the Holy Spirit and still heed the landmarks marking the horizons of our own personal background and experience.

I had to face this challenge myself, and I can hardly describe my gratitude to God, for His grace and favor led me to a pathway that allowed me to broaden my boundaries without disrespecting the landmarks of my heritage. Let me tell you how this happened.

Broadening Beyond a Restrictive Viewpoint

I suppose I was taught the same way most Christians are. Almost all of us are presented with a restrictive view of speaking with tongues. Whether our background trained us to accept this on *our* terms or to reject this on almost *any* terms, the viewpoint from which we're first oriented lays boundaries in our souls. Like ancient landmarks, an aura of authority rooted in traditions or forged by our esteemed mentors can hold an awesome sway over our attitudes toward tongues. Whatever our restriction (mine was accepting, but tied to a doctrinaire mandate), such landmarks become boundaries. They have a profound ability to restrain our sense of freedom to explore God's Word or answer the Spirit's call beyond our family-imposed red lines.

Perhaps nothing has restricted the vision of the beauty of spiritual language more than reactions to the historic doctrinal posturing of pentecostals like myself. As readily as I want to honor my pentecostal forbearers for preserving the testimony of tongues and for generating a passion for Spirit-fullness among millions, at the same time I confess that I believe an unintended but nonetheless restrictive barrier was built. I think this obstacle has become a roadblock to growth in two ways: (1) It has often blocked pentecostal-charismatics from discerning the *scope* of the spiritual language's use, and (2) It has blocked most non-charismatics from seeing the *real* purposes of spiritual language. Consequently, the discussion or debate over tongues has usually started at the wrong place. I am referring to a classical Pentecostal conviction: the historic tradition that requires tongues as "the evidence," verifying the validity, of a person's being baptized in the Spirit. It was a sincerely begotten dogma, never intended to alienate, limit, or restrict. But it has restricted, and it may help us to understand how this dogma came about.

Around the turn of the twentieth century, my spiritual ancestors in the Pentecostal movement had all been summarily dismissed from their traditional Protestant denominations after and because they had experienced speaking with tongues. Their entry into this experience had been entirely wholesome and holy in motivation. They were godly people, hungering only for more of God's power in their lives—the same spiritual passion that has always preceded revival and visitations of the Holy Spirit. And their hunger had been rewarded: an Acts 2, Pentecost-like visitation from God broke out in many places around the world and spread rapidly![1]

When this visitation was impugned and they were castigated for their experience, they took an understandably defensive stance in contending for their biblical experience of God's power. Searching the Scriptures, they found sufficient instances of tongues occurring simultaneously with people receiving or being baptized in the Holy Spirit, so they framed doctrinal statements based on these texts. Their experience of *how* these New Testament gifts and power were recovered governed their interpretation. They concluded: "Speaking with tongues is the initial, physical evidence of the Baptism with the Holy Spirit." What had been a pathway of discovery for their own lives, was thereby forged into an inviolable rule; in effect, demanding that anyone who would claim to be filled with the Holy Spirit *must* speak with tongues. For them, not to speak with tongues equaled not to have been filled with the Spirit. (Their convictions ran *so* deep that some people mistakenly thought pentecostals believed that a non-tongues-speaker wasn't even saved, but this has *never* been the belief of any mainstream pentecostals or charismatics.)

Countering the initial-evidence requirement posed by pentecostals, critics pointed to other instances in the Scriptures where people received the infilling of the Holy Spirit where no mention is made of speaking with tongues. Because the spirit of debate was already in control, arguments tended to deepen the chasm between good people. In time, anyone unwilling to swear to the initial-evidence dogma was judged by pentecostals like me to have failed the test of doctrinal purity regarding the fullness or the baptism, while their opponents built structures of equally dogmatic opposition to *everything* in the tongues package. So it was, years later, I found myself called as a pastor and struggling in this milieu with these countering dogmas. It brought me to my own travail with landmarks and boundaries.

My struggle was never over the value or desirability of speaking with tongues. Once I realized their place and contribution to my experience, I only saw them as desirable—as scripturally practical and purposeful. But I labored with questions as to how they applied from a doctrinal perspective. Having been trained in a Pentecostal college, and my pastoral work having always been among pentecostals, it hardly occurred to me to question the doctrine early on. It was a closed subject: Tongues were the first evidence of the Spirit-filled life. I knew the biblical case; one which by any criteria an honest student will admit is there to be made. If you wish to proof text an initial-physical-evidence-as-tongues proposition, a case can be made and argued on biblical grounds.

However, I was coming to see—integrity with the Word forcing me to confess—that it is equally true that a conclusive, airtight case could *not* be categorically proven. In fact, I saw that either side of the argument could succeed in forming a biblical-grounds dogma on the relationship between tongues and the fullness of the Holy Spirit. Whether one showed the texts to prove it true or those to prove it false, you could stand your ground and use the Bible as evidence to make your case.

There *is* a frequent relationship—seeming almost to be related in a cause ("being filled") and effect ("speaking with tongues") dynamic. On the other hand, honesty with *all* the Word forces another acknowledgment. Maybe God didn't intend us to isolate tongues as a proof of anything; perhaps He had something greater in mind for tongues than their merely being an evidence. I was having to face my own unperceived prejudice, for I suddenly found myself hurled by the hand of God into the middle of a miracle. Something overwhelming—something virtually incredible to me was bursting forth at the church I was pastoring.

Nothing has more impacted the shape of my whole experience than the tremendous visitation of God's might and mercy which came two decades ago to our small congregation at The First Foursquare Church of Van Nuys, better known today as The Church on the Way. Almost overnight, I was surrounded with such a surge of God's sovereign workings, I was humbled before Him. Over the first two or three years, the Holy Spirit drew me to honestly and humbly reevaluate and thereby refine my views on many aspects of those truths undergirding the life of Christ's church and to freshly assess the keys to vital New Testament life.

- Not until now had I caught a glimpse of the glorious power waiting to be released amid congregational worship. It awakened me to the Holy Spirit's call to lead people to a childlike humility before God, and to do so with a renewed sense of the priestly dimension in New Testament praise (1 Pet. 2:5, 9).

- I began to see the importance of utter transparency in personal and corporate relationships as the essence of meaning behind the Spirit's call to "walk in the light" (1 John 1:6–10). Seeing this, I was drawn to a far more open method of teaching the Bible, becoming far more available to self-disclosure and confession of my own learning process under God's grace.

- The Spirit of God began to lead me toward a far greater simplicity in evangelistic endeavor. I was turned around— and thereby my style was transformed from what I would call "promoting the gospel." I discovered a far more fruitful and less "sweaty" approach as Ephesians 4:11–16 came to life. I'd call it the edify-the-body-and-watch-it-multiply-itself method.

Among these transforming lessons, and not the least of my own "awakenings," was my coming to terms with the question, "What is the sign of the infilling of the Holy Spirit?" For me, a pentecostal, this posed a real dilemma as I was confronted by doctrines which dictated inflexibility. And I had strong relationships within my denomination—ones which could intimidate and dilute my will to be refined and taught by the Lord.

Still, I knew I couldn't proceed on the pathway of full renewal unless I was willing to remain shapable under the Holy Spirit's dealings. I was facing a case of landmarks, and trying to find the way to broadened boundaries without sacrificing respect for the monuments raised in faith by spiritual fathers—those godly leaders of an earlier generation who had sired me in the blessing I knew.

Signs of the Holy Spirit's Fullness

My first concern was to begin by settling the question, "What is the Bible's sign of Holy Spirit fullness?" It's an entirely proper one for any Christian to ask. After all, we *ought* to want to know we have met God in a verifiable and biblically acceptable way. But for anyone seeking the right answers, two immediate problems rise. First, there is a multiplicity of signs shown in the Word; how shall we prioritize them? Second, there is a human tendency to formulate a ritual around every operation of divine grace; how can we avoid that? Perhaps the best beginning point is to start by looking at three very clear, commonly agreed upon signs.

1. With regard to signs of the Holy Spirit's fullness, everyone acknowledges that *love* is the first and foremost we should expect.

   - Love is the essence of God's nature (1 John 4:16).

   - Love is the first-on-the-list fruit of the Holy Spirit (Gal. 5:22–23).

- Paul appeals to love-above-all when writing the Corinthians; adjusting their perspective on and their practice
  of the miraculous sign of tongues (1 Corinthians 13).

2. Next, few will challenge the proposal that if love is first,
   surely power must be the second sign we would anticipate,
   for Jesus said:

   > You shall receive power when the Holy Spirit has come upon
   > you; and you shall be witnesses to *Me*.
   >   Acts 1:8

   - Holy Spirit fullness *is* to expand our ability to become
     vibrant, living evidences of the resurrected Christ.

   - The Holy Spirit *is* given to us to exalt Jesus in and
     through us so that others may be drawn to Jesus Christ
     the Lord.

3. A third arena of expectation may be found in the entire
   list of "signs" in 1 Corinthians 12:8–10. The nine gifts
   listed there are revealed as the unique domain of the Holy
   Spirit Himself. Additionally, the full complement of the
   nine fruits listed in Galatians 5:22–23 are reasonable expectations to be manifested as traits of His character working in us. As often is said, His incoming with power would
   certainly recommend the idea that at least one of His gifts
   may become manifest in the one being filled. And if He is
   indeed present in fullness, fruit becoming His personality
   would at least be expected in a "budding" stage!

With all the above as valid, biblical evidences, there is good reason why
any emphasis on *one* gift might be questioned. Who could dare insist
on an absolute requirement that tongues be an ironclad rule—a demanded sign to verify the infilling of the Holy Spirit?

But Then, Too . . .

On the other hand, as I honestly weighed all this, I was still finding consistent results as I encouraged people to *expect* to speak with
tongues when they asked the Lord Jesus Christ to fill them with the
Holy Spirit and power. Of course, I had originally been motivated to

do this for doctrinal reasons, believing tongues were mandated. But though my convictions as to a "mandate" were waning, there still seemed an apparent willingness of the Lord to respond in grace, however imperfect my view may have been. Regularly, people met Jesus in a mighty way—in overflowing fullness. And even though tongues were never forced on anyone, the unthreatening atmosphere of expectation resulted in virtually all receiving a spiritual language at the same time they were filled.

Because there are at least three biblical cases of this sign being manifested in this way, I didn't feel I was on shallow grounds. At Pentecost (Acts 2:4), at Cornelius' house (Acts 10:44–48), and at Ephesus (Acts 19:6), the sign of speaking with tongues plainly accompanies people's receiving their initial infilling of the Holy Spirit. But I still couldn't rest in the notion that God's intent in this sign was being properly understood. Was it meant as a proof? Or rather, was it meant as a provision?

I was beginning to suspect the latter was the issue, that tongues had been given as a divine provision—a beneficial resource, always available where faith-without-fear was ready to receive and exercise the spiritual language. The undeniable breadth revealed in the Scriptures, along with the inescapable evidence throughout the Christian community, was forcing me from my doctrinal posturing.

My first decisive steps began with what, for me, was to risk appearing to compromise by deciding to admit the obvious. There were (and are) too many people whom I know living power-filled lives under the touch and gifts of the Holy Spirit, though never having spoken with tongues. I determined to cease contending for another definition of their fullness and to refuse to deny their anointed ministry as being other than fully Spirit-filled. But as surely as to deny that would have been dishonest, it would have been equally unwise for me to retreat from what I was discovering of tongues as a provision for all believers—for prayer and praise.

Proven results in my own ministry evidenced people almost always receiving spiritual language when they welcomed the fullness of the Spirit into their lives. I had no reason to cease teaching this expectation, but how was I to merge these two convictions I was reaching?

1. I was convinced I couldn't *demand* tongues as an evidence of Holy-Spirit-fullness; and

2. I was convinced I couldn't *deny* the availability or value of tongues if welcomed by those seeking His fullness.

Let me share how subtle bonds of restricting prejudice were undone and how a grand release was discovered.

Free from an Unrequired Mission

I laugh at myself today. It seems so peculiar that it had never occurred to me before! But the greatest step in my release came when I saw something so obvious, I was humbled not to have seen it sooner. It happened when these words dawned on me one day in a moment of liberating insight: **God hasn't called me to tell people whether or not the Lord Jesus Christ has baptized them with the Holy Spirit!**

What a relief!

That one concept—and the decision to live within its manifest wisdom—completely removed the need *ever* to debate again, ever to argue *any* doctrinal position on the subject. May I affirm that here—to you, dear reader—just as I affirm it everywhere today.

I do urge believers in Christ to welcome the Holy Spirit's fullness and to follow Jesus in His life and power! And I do hope and pray they will be receptive to and become functional in the spiritual language available to them. But I have no disposition whatever to propose a doctrinal position on anyone, or to require a "tongues" experience of them—you, me, anyone—to validate anything of our place in Christ or our walk with Him. Please see and believe that! For the beauty of spiritual language can only clearly be seen and received for all its precious worth when our eyes are unfogged by vision-blurring debate or demands. I believe the simple evidence in God's Word is that He never intended spiritual language as a proof, but that He has offered it as a provision—a resource for readiness in prayer and praise.

Finding this liberating perspective, I made a pastoral choice within our own congregation. We chose to continue urging those to whom we ministered to *expect* to speak with tongues when they receive the fullness of the Spirit. We still do. But it is (1) always encouraged in an environment of faith, and (2) never pressured as a requirement for spiritual acceptance of one's experience in God.

This path of ministry was and is borne of the simple conviction that since the church was given this birthright at its inception, it is verifiably available today, and that in God's own time everyone may expect this blessed prayer and praise resource. We refuse to be separated from Christians holding other views, but it is admittedly a joyous thing to see the large numbers of believers from every background, who freely enter into the exercise of the spiritual language.

There's a reason that we see so many who do enter into spiritual language. It's not that they're coerced, nor are they made to feel inferior if they do not speak with tongues. But in time, virtually all to whom we minister do, for the simple reason that *they believe this potential belongs to every believer.* This is a viewpoint we foster, and we believe there is a strong biblical basis for such a peace-filled, confident expectancy; an unpressured, but unhesitant spirit of receptive faith.

The derivation of our conviction goes back to two simple facts: (1) that Jesus Himself initiated the subject of spiritual language; and (2) the Father Himself designed for the church to be born with it as a birthright.

The Author of the Subject

May I begin by underscoring one fact above all others about the matter of spiritual language: **Jesus is the One who introduced the subject of spiritual language.** I think that fact is important—that it very much deserves and needs to sink into the collective mind-set of the church.

Some years ago, my sister was talking with her pastor, a dear man who pastored a rather staid evangelical church in Minnesota. He knew of Luanne's charismatic experience and accepted her with Christian grace. But one day, as they conversed on the topic, the pastor said, "Even if God did give me one of the gifts"—then he grimaced, and continued—"I certainly wouldn't want it to be tongues!" Without malice, my sister gently asked, "Pastor, did you just hear yourself?" He looked at her, quizzically, and she went on: "You just spoke in a very demeaning way of one of the gifts of God, the Holy Spirit."

The godly man, suddenly jarred by the recognition of the slap-in-God's-face flippancy borne of a prejudiced past, reflectively and repentantly responded: "My! I suppose that doesn't sound very good, does it? Lord, forgive me." His honest acknowledgment was prompted by the reminder that tongues are God's idea. In fact, no one less than our dear Savior Himself first spoke of tongues; promising this blessing to His disciples:

> And these signs will follow those who believe: In My name they will . . . speak with new tongues.
>
> Mark 16:17

That's where tongues—spiritual language—starts in the New Testament. And at its first mention, this miraculous language of prayer and praise is the *first* sign among the five Jesus mentions in this text. Interestingly enough, it's also the first of His prophesied signs to actually be fulfilled, being manifested on the very day the church was born (Acts 2:4).

Perhaps we should pause here, again.

As with the reminder that Jesus is the first to mention speaking with tongues, there is a second remarkably important fact related to their first occurrence. Would you note with me something too easily overlooked? Yet the profound simplicity and crystal clarity of this fact says something about the Father's view of the spiritual language: *The church began speaking with tongues the same day it came into being!* That's a fact worthy of a special place in our heart's understanding, seeing our heavenly Father, the Living God Himself, was the sole designer and sovereign instigator of Pentecost's events.

Since this is so, can we not on those grounds alone capture something of heaven's point of view concerning the relative worth or desirability of tongues? The Father certainly wouldn't have allowed anything unworthy, unlovely, or unloving to accidentally happen. Speaking with tongues didn't just crowd in on its own, as though man forced an arbitrary Johnny-come-lately sign upon the church's birth and into the church's origins. Neither was this spiritual language an embarrassing surprise to the Almighty! Rather, the supernatural gift of language was given for holy and wholesome purposes, and He allowed it because He created it and completely endorses it. Perhaps we can all afford to be reminded: Tongues—spiritual language—is God's idea!

- Jesus prophesied it.
- The Father intended it.
- The Holy Spirit enabled it.
- The church received it.

The spiritual language *must* be important or it wouldn't have been given this place at the church's inception.

So, since God authored this exercise, what did He have in mind?

It was an incredible, indescribably beautiful thing that day the church was born, as supernatural praises to God wafted from the tongues of those being filled with His Holy Spirit. Psalm 133 seems to have forecast what happened:

> Behold, how good and how pleasant it is for brethren to dwell to-
> gether in unity! . . . For there the Lord commanded the bless-
> ing—Life forevermore!
>
> Psalm 133:1, 3

As that small clutch of saints gathered according to Jesus' command, awaiting the Holy Spirit's power from on high, their unity was molded in prayer until they came into one accord. Then and there—that day so long ago—the Lord *did* command the blessing. And as the blessing overflowed them, they realized a new God-given privilege; the right to an expression of new worship and praise which was released by the Holy Spirit's presence and enablement. And notice that when it first appeared, spiritual language was not given sparingly: "They were *all* filled . . . and began to speak with other tongues."

At the church's birth this "birthright" was everyone's!

The ability to worship and praise God at a new, transcendent dimension was universal that day, a fact that argues more for its universal continuance than for its dismissal as a unique phenomenon only once intended.

There were no comparisons made that day—no competition felt between fellow Christians. These problems only occur where dear people, who both love Jesus Christ, have been taught to argue with one another over the desirability, the value, or even the continued propriety of this Holy-Spirit-given language.

My heartfelt desire in urging a welcoming of this refreshing, praiseful expression is borne of this evidence that *all* were mutual sharers at the start—*all* entered into something manifestly a part of every believer's privilege in prayer.

Remember how Jacob was commended for prizing the birthright, the benefits of the firstborn, while Esau disregarded and later despised them? Similarly, it seems, some treasure this resource while others disregard it. But why should any of us be hesitant or embarrassed for seeking a prayer and praise resource which the Father created, blessed, and gave to the whole church at her beginning?

If the Lord was unhesitant to give spiritual language as a part of the broad arena of blessings for Spirit-filled life and service, we have no reason to be less than ready in opening to it. *You* aren't—*I'm* not—*we* aren't losing our perspective on godly priorities when we, as Christians, desire today what every believer was originally given at the start. The spiritual language is not a reserved resource for a select few.

But Do All Speak with Tongues?

It's right to ask this question, too. Paul asked it of the Corinthians, and the text makes clear that his rhetorical question expected no for an answer:

> Are all apostles? Are all prophets? Are all teachers? Are all workers of miracles?
> Do all have gifts of healings? Do all speak with tongues? Do all interpret?
>
> 1 Corinthians 12:29–30

That passage and its context would seem to close the question if mere convenience were all we sought. That is, if we simply want to avoid ever expecting or having to deal with spiritual language, we can lay it here and excuse ourselves with the quick snap of a single proof text. But if we do, we not only will leave the subject half dealt with, we also may be removing a holy, worthwhile expectation from people who would welcome this beautiful blessing if they could be satisfied that it is freely and fully available to them.

The "No, all do *not* speak with tongues," clearly implied in 1 Corinthians 12:30, needs the biblical balancing point provided it in 1 Corinthians 14. Otherwise, the beauty of *all* the truth about the exercise of "tongues" remains veiled—only half-told. And once we have removed the strain of a doctrinaire demand from over our heads, as I sought to earlier, it can become beautifully rewarding to simply, without pressure, look at the possibility of the availability to all believers of a spiritual language for prayer and praise.

A starting place, which seems to have helped thousands as I've shared about the beauty of spiritual language, has been in my beginning with a definition of the objective in 1 Corinthians 12–14. First, look at the summary purpose of each chapter.

1. Chapter 12—The *Gifts of the Spirit* is the subject, with a special emphasis on the unique way the Holy Spirit wills to use each of us in different ways.

2. Chapter 13—The *Spirit of the Gifts* is the theme, especially noting how love is to be the controlling spirit in exercising *all* the gifts throughout *all* the church.

3. Chapter 14—The *Language of the Spirit* is the issue, as the writer urges order in the exercise of the gifts of tongues

and prophecy, noting the difference between public and private use of the spiritual language.

This overview is important because by distinguishing the focus of each segment of Paul's discourse, it's easier to see why he says two different things about speaking with tongues.

1. In 1 Corinthians 12:30, he indicates "*not* all" will speak with tongues.
2. In 1 Corinthians 14:5, he says, "I wish you all" *did* speak with tongues.

Would the apostle express his "wish" for all (*thelo*, "to desire, to will, to prefer, to intend")[2] if he believed the "not all" was a closed case? This apparent paradox is soon resolved if we note the different objective of the two passages. (Please take time to think this through with your Bible opened.)

• The *first* reference (12:30) relates to tongues as one of the nine gifts. In that regard Paul explains its proper use: It is a public exercise (14:26) that will edify the church (14:12–13) when the requirement of interpretation is faithfully observed (14:27–28).

• The *second* reference (14:5) appears at the beginning of Paul's distinguishing the *public* prophetic use of tongues (when interpreted) from the *private* edifying benefit they may provide. In this sorting out process, he explains the personal use of tongues; for edifying the believer (14:4) in times of private praise, prayer, and worship of God (14:2).

To distinguish between the public and private employment of tongues I often used the terms "gift" of tongues and "grace" of tongues. I use the term "grace" to remind us of the broad, generous availability of this prayer language. It is freely available as a resource to any or every believer who will receive it—just as all did at the beginning.[3] I employ the term, the "grace of tongues," in contrast to the "gift of tongues," because of Paul's distinguishing between a publicly exercised (14:26) and privately employed use of tongues (14:5a, 18). Thus, the spiritual language, as a personal resource for every believer who wishes it, is differentiated from the "gift" intended as a ministry-to-others resource. In this way, the spiritual language in one's private experience is not linked to a doctrine, but to a divine availability—to be received by grace and through faith—subject to personal choice.

Of course, *all* operations of the Holy Spirit are "by grace through faith—subject to personal choice." Still, understandably, someone asks, "But aren't the gifts of the Spirit, including tongues and interpretation at *His* choice—'as He wills' (12:11)?" And the answer is yes. Their operation should be *welcomed*, but they cannot be *willed*. But in stark, biblical contrast, look how Paul's description of the ongoing exercise of one's spiritual language clearly leaves it to the individual's discretion. He says,

> "*I will* pray . . . *I will* sing with the Spirit."
>   1 Corinthians 14:15

We can be sure Paul is not usurping the Holy Spirit's initiative! Rather, he is demonstrating by his own example the fact that a distinct difference between the "gift" and the "grace" of spiritual language is present in the manifestations of tongues. And he shows the spiritual language to be at the disposal of any believer who may choose to receive and employ it.

Again, may we see how:

• The "gift" of tongues is (1) limited in distribution (1 Cor. 12:11, 30), and (2) its public exercise is to be closely governed (1 Cor. 14:27–28); while

• The "grace" of tongues is so broadly available that Paul wishes that "all" enjoyed its blessing (1 Cor. 14:5a); blessing which includes the benefits of (1) distinctive communication with God (1 Cor. 14:2); (2) edifying of the believer's private life (1 Cor. 14:4); and (3) worship and thanksgiving with beauty and propriety (1 Cor. 14:15–17).

Question: Isn't self-edification selfish?

Answer: No, it isn't. Self-edification is a spiritual process of being built up in the inner man, not puffed up with human pride. This is confirmed by Jude's words: "But you, beloved, build yourselves up on your most holy faith, praying in the Holy Spirit" (Jude 20).

Question: What is the difference in the language aspect of the "gift" and the "grace" of tongues?

Answer: None that we know, only that the first is always to be interpreted. We are shown two different sides of a similar phenomenon. Both involve tongues, so their similarity is in the supernatural *nature* of both: the gift of tongues (with interpretation supernaturally ministering exhortation, edification, and comfort to others) and the grace of tongues (by private prayer supernaturally enabling worship, praise, and intercession).

The difference between these operations of the Holy Spirit is: (1) *not every* Christian has reason to expect he or she will necessarily exercise the public "gift"; while (2) *any* Christian may expect and welcome the private "grace" of spiritual language in his or her personal time of prayer fellowship *with* God (1 Cor. 14:2), praiseful worship *before* God (1 Cor. 14:15–17), and intercessory prayer *to* God (Rom. 8:26–27).

Question: Doesn't Paul say that the gift of prophecy is preferred over tongues?

Answer: In 1 Corinthians 14:5, after affirming "I wish you all spoke with tongues," the apostle teaches the preferred desirability of prophecy for edifying the church when it is assembled. Though he adds that a person's exercise of spiritual language should not substitute for growth in prophesying, this does not diminish the sincerity of his earlier expressed wish.

We'll be looking at prophesying in a moment, as well as examining the broader values and benefits of our private use of the spiritual language. But here, the point is to note with clarity the distinction drawn between tongues as a gift which will not be exercised by all Christians and tongues as a grace which may be exercised by any Christian.

Is tongues a birthright of every believer, an experience which may be fully welcomed, actuated, and applied in biblical order as any individual Christian prayerfully and humbly may desire this from God? I think the Word says so. I think this truth is present in comparing 1 Corinthians 12 and 14. **But I also think it will only remain "beautiful" as an applied truth to the degree that we always remember 1 Corinthians 13!** It is in the spirit of a mutual devotion to the best interests of one another—1 Corinthians 13, the Love Chapter—that the apostle Paul gives us the insight and the invitation to a daily, prayer-use of the spiritual language in 1 Corinthians 14. He knows, as we all do, that when the "perfect is come"—that is, the ultimate appearance of Christ and His Kingdom—"tongues shall cease" (1 Corinthians 13). But until that day they are desirable for ongoing use.[4]

- That explains why Paul would "wish" spiritual language for all believers (1 Cor. 14:5).

- That helps us understand why he so readily expressesed his own *abounding* employment of the spiritual language in his prayer life (1 Cor. 14:18).

- It also clearly shows why the apostle ordered *against* there ever being a prohibitive posturing toward tongues (1 Cor. 14:39).

Here then, tongues are a common grace, beside and separate from the gift, a dimension of speaking with tongues that might be exercised by all believers—or at least by any or as many of us who would also "wish" we spoke with tongues.

The settling of the matter of the viable privilege of any believer to receive the spiritual language *without* a doctrinal demand removed a sticky issue I had to face and wrestle with. The Word of God removed confusion and competition; it resolved complexity and brought clarity, love, and simplicity to the subject of tongues.

I have found other Christian friends helped as I have been by this realization—indeed, they felt relieved! When this biblically sound, spiritually liberating approach is unfolded, every Christian is free to respond to the spiritual language with a loving absence of doctrinal conditions. It gives place to the possibility of a holy hunger rising, to welcome a heavenly resource available to them, rather than a debate or doctrine being imposed on them. For my part, I still strongly encourage people to welcome spiritual language at the time they openheartedly ask Jesus to fill them with the Holy Spirit. Again, I do *not* present tongues as a required proof but encourage all to welcome this as a privilege.

Then too, other Christians who believe they have already been filled with the Spirit might find a happy expectancy in the truth we've discussed here. The ready availability of the spiritual language, as an expanded possibility for their own private prayer life, may be welcomed for the value it offers and the blessings it includes.

What a liberation! Once speaking with tongues ceases to be seen as limited or as a demand, the beauty of this spiritual language can be seen and received, according to its gracious offer—in the spirit of God's love and according to one's desire.

Breaking Free in Fullness and Fellowship

Something freeing had happened to me! It affected our congregation's life, and the wave of love which rose as we opened to the Holy Spirit seemed to increase—enveloping people from all parts of the Body of Christ. Though I had never recognized my need for the Lord's refining my views on Spirit-fullness, the rising of God's workings among us came like waves of an incoming tide, oversweeping the residue of my hitherto unperceived sectarianism.

In the end, I neither denied the roots of my denominational relationship (for we live in the benefits of spiritual language without making it a law) nor allowed respected landmarks to become restrictive boundaries. Fellowship was strengthened through a spirit of respectful submission, and beyond the immediate circle of my denomination fellowship, something lovely blossomed and grew. An ever-broadening circle of ever-deepening relationships began to appear everywhere. A liberated perspective allowed new appreciation for the broad diversity throughout the whole church. Now, if anyone felt reticent about the matter of speaking with tongues—even if he or she felt resistant!—it was now impossible for me to feel offended. I was relieved of any need to argue my case and freed to respond to earnest inquirers without imposing a doctrine—merely encouraging a privilege. Yes!

In much the same way, several new landmarks of love are being erected. A sweeping move of the Spirit of God's grace is bringing a readiness to receive one another in joyous fellowship and mutual Christian love. And in that environment, fresh streams of worship are being unlocked as the Lord Himself commands the blessing!

He's doing it for a reason.

He wants us all to hear what the Spirit is saying to the churches. And through that living Body—His church—Jesus is rising in resurrection power to speak to a world with penetrating strength and prophetic life.

7

For You May All Prophesy

"In the last days . . . on all flesh . . . your sons, daughters, young and old, men and women," was the time and scope of the promise: it's now and it's us.

*T*he little sanctuary only seated fifty people, so as small as the Sunday evening attendance of a dozen worshipers may have been, it seemed like a "crowd" for a wintry night. So as I stood to open the Word of God and minister to our fledgling congregation—a small mission work that was hardly a year old, I felt good. Only a few months before there was nothing, but now a little church was beginning to appear, and on this Sunday night the preacher was excited. There were *people* present, and I had a good message prepared to feed the tiny flock.

You might imagine my dismay, however, when less than three minutes into my sermon, two heads had already lurched forward in sleep and there seemed only measured responsiveness from the glazed eyes of those who were dutifully listening to their young pastor. At the moment I didn't feel especially discerning, but I did sense that something was happening here beyond natural explanation. I may not have been the greatest young preacher since Charles Spurgeon, but I knew I wasn't boring, and the deadness of the formal, churchy response—replete with snoozing saints—was not something I could disregard.

Without displaying displeasure or irritation with the people, I simply stopped my message. "Folks," I gently said, addressing the group who were all older than me by at least eight to ten years, "I really think we need to stop and pray."

If I had had any idea of what was about to happen I probably wouldn't have had the nerve to begin this prayer, because the opening months of this little congregation's experience had involved almost nothing of what might be called pentecostal or charismatic activity.

These were days before the revival of the 1970s, which stirred the church on every continent with an awareness and new openness to New Testament-type church life. And here in the church-planting endeavor, as convinced as Anna and I were of the validity of our Spirit-filled experience, we knew little about how to transmit it to others. Although we had been well trained in God's Word at LIFE Bible College, at that time, peculiarly enough, many pentecostals themselves had waned in their convictions. There seemed to be a suspicion of the supernatural, and in many schools little was done to foster faith's expectation for New Testament power; that is, beyond the proper wisdom of seeking to win the lost through evangelism.

But this night, everyone present had already been born again—we had led them to Christ. And they were people who were willing to grow—their presence at Sunday night's service, which was "extracurricular" to most others, seemed to verify that. But nothing—I mean *nothing* was happening in *this* service!

Until I stopped.

Until I said, almost despairingly, "Let's pray."

I had no sooner closed my eyes to do so when an indescribable blackness began to churn like a cloudy veil before my inner vision. I had never experienced anything like this before, and at the immediate moment did not realize I was having my first experience in receiving a "word"—a prophetic picture-type message. What I *did* realize was what this ugliness, this seething blackness represented: sin. It certainly wasn't sin in a casual sense, but neither was it sin in any specific sense. Rather, it was plainly and awfully the grotesqueness of sin, sin in its suffocating power to blind, to swallow up, to block the blessedness of the beauty of a soul's vision of God. At that moment, I didn't have time to think of or reflect on 2 Corinthians 4:4, but afterward I related this picture to Paul's description of the darkness sin brings to human understanding: "Whose minds the god of this age has blinded, who do not believe, lest the light of the gospel of the glory of Christ, who is the image of God, should shine on them."

What happened wasn't a reasoned response to that text, but the passion that stirred my actions at that moment were that I *did*, dramatically and intuitively, sense the intensity of our adversary's work in keeping people from capturing a glimpse of all that the Lord Jesus has for them.

I had only begun my prayer with the words, "Lord God, I pray that . . . ," when the vision burst over my awareness like a sudden storm. As it did, I could only begin to tremble with a sense of the horror of sins' blinding capability. So I paused briefly, to gain composure, and then continued with the words ". . . that You would help us see . . ."

Then it happened.

The word exploded from my lips: "Sin!"

That single word rumbled up from out of my deepest being, breaking over my lips with a force that shocked me. I virtually bellowed it. Just once. But the effect was staggering to everyone present: "Sin!" I cried out, almost as if pained by the word itself.

Knowing the shock to the people would be great (though I had calculated none of this and hardly knew what to do myself), I lifted my head after having uttered the word "sin" so explosively. Unsurprisingly, every head had snapped upward to look at me—stunned amazement written on every face! No one was asleep now!

Looking into their wide-eyed countenances, an uncharacteristic boldness possessed me: I pointed straight at those in the pews and ordered, "Bow your heads!" And just as quickly as every head had snapped upward to see what was happening to their young pastor, each head snapped back downward in awed reverence before a power they felt in the room.

It is difficult for me to tell this story today without being caught up with a holy laughter:

- laughter at how God shook us all awake, for what followed impacted more than the two who had fallen asleep;

- laughter at how God laid hold of me, for until that moment I had been the model of what I thought pulpit propriety ought to be;

- laughter at how the people responded, for their heads had bobbed up and down so rapidly in a tandem response to my declarations of "Sin!" and "Bow your heads!" that the memory prompts an irrepressible chuckle (with praise to the Lord that no one suffered whiplash!).

But what made the moment most memorable wasn't the shock of any human being's behavior, it was the Holy Spirit's presence. It was the unforgettable onset of a genuine spiritual awakening for a season in that small congregation's life.

As heads had resumed a posture of prayer, I stepped from the platform and strode back and forth declaiming the horrendous nature of
sin's blinding power and calling us to let God move on our hearts until
His light would burn out any darkness. I hadn't spoken for two minutes when I gave directions: "I want every man to come to the altar
area and pray. Each woman, turn and kneel where you are and call on
the Lord." It was as though buttons had been punched in heaven, issuing electric jolts to everyone in the room. The people couldn't respond fast enough. The men virtually leaped to their feet and hurried
forward to kneel. The women seemed to spin from their seated position to a kneeling one. And the room was vibrating with an aliveness
unbegotten by man.

Other than the strong time of prayer that followed, there were no
particular signs and there was very little emotion other than a sense of
joyfulness and awe at the presence of a holy reality. We prayed, repented, sang, praised God, and read the Scriptures which the event
brought to mind. It was glorious.

However, after the meeting had concluded and Anna and I had
returned to the parsonage, I felt concerned about the impact of the
upheaval the evening had registered. As we snacked and talked together
at home, I said to her, "Honey, I wonder what's going to happen now.
The people have never seen anything like this. What will they think
about it when they get home? Do you think they might decide it's only
fanaticism—and never come again?"

The demonstration we had experienced was new to us in terms of
our own leadership, though we had both witnessed God genuinely at
work in such unusual ways before. But this transcended anything I had
ever imagined myself doing, and it certainly didn't fit into the neatly
packaged brand of church life that we had presented here . . . until
that night. What would happen? It wasn't long until my question was
answered.

The phone bounced off the hook all Monday morning.

People who hadn't been present were the first to call. For example,
"Dorothy and Earl just called and told us what a wonderful service you
had last night! They said it was absolutely thrilling—that God was there
in a deep and powerful way!" Others called who had been there, simply to review the meeting and to express their gratitude to God . . .
and to me. It was that last part, their thanks to me, that was hard to
receive, because I was more aware than anyone that I had nothing to
do with it. In fact, if God had warned me in advance, I must confess

with embarrassment that at that time in my ministry I probably would have been tempted to opt out. But as it occurred, it became not only a time of opening the door to God's grace in the life of that small congregation, it also became the beginning point of my realizing, at a distinct dimension, the purpose and power of the Holy Spirit's work in prophecy. What do I mean by "prophecy"?

The Spirit of Prophecy

The simplest meaning of "prophesy" is to "speak forth" or to "foretell." The blend of this dual idea was most commonly found among the Hebrew prophets who (1) would foresee through prophetic vision what God was about to do, and then (2) would tell forth this "word," calling for appropriate action on the part of the people. Of course, the Bible contains many of their prophecies—ones which have been fulfilled and ones that yet await fulfillment. And it is clear that those contained in the sacred Scriptures have been placed there under the inspiration of the Holy Spirit, Who has intended them to be a part of the permanent pages of the closed canon of the Bible—the Eternal Word of God. But there were other operations of the gift of prophecy in both the Old and New Testament as well; exercisings of this gift which make clear that the giving of Scripture was not intended to be the only way the Spirit of prophecy works.

Perhaps the most pivotal texts as to God's desire and intent for this gift are found in Numbers 11 and in Acts 2. It is in these two places (one in each Testament) that the revelation and the realization of God's desire for prophecy are clearly taught.

In the first passage, Moses appeals to the Lord, acknowledging the fact that his hierarchical place of sole leadership of the people was more than he could bear (Num. 11:11–15). In response, God spoke to Moses:

> Gather to Me seventy men of the elders of Israel, whom you know; . . . bring them to the tabernacle of meeting, that they may stand there with you. Then I will come down and talk with you there. I will take of the Spirit that is upon you and will put the same upon them.
>
> Numbers 11:16–17

As the morning dawns, the elders assembled as the Lord directed, and the Bible says: "Then the Lord came down in the cloud . . . [and]

when the Spirit rested upon them, they prophesied" (v. 25). However, the absence of two of the seventy—who for some reason were detained when the visitation took place—introduces a very significant insight. Even though the two men, Eldad and Medad, were not at the Tabernacle where the elders had been called to assemble, they both still experienced the Holy Spirit coming upon them at the place they were in the Israelite camp, and they *also* prophesied! When Joshua heard of this, he hurried to Moses to express his alarm. It was as though he was disstressed with something that seemed out of control. But Moses' response is different. In a characteristic, self-effacing, God-honoring sensitivity, he exclaims to Joshua:

> Are you zealous for my sake? Oh, that all the Lord's people were prophets and that the Lord would put His Spirit upon them!
> Numbers 11:29

As the *Spirit-Filled Life Bible* comments on this text: "Joshua apparently wants to control. Though Eldad and Medad were legitimate elders, they were not present at the tabernacle. The Spirit is not confined to particular persons, but is free to rest upon whom He wills. This met with the approval of Moses, who desired a democratization of the Spirit and envisioned a nation of prophets."[1]

Further in the pages of God's Word, the Holy Spirit which not only stirred such hope in Moses, but Who preserved his words for our later instruction, inspired Joel with more than hope. He moved this prophet to announce the promise of the possibility of *all* God's people prophesying.

> And it shall come to pass afterward that I will pour out My Spirit on all flesh; your sons and your daughters shall prophesy, your old men shall dream dreams, your young men shall see visions, and also on My menservants and on My maidservants I will pour out My Spirit in those days.
> Joel 2:28–29

Even later, this is precisely the text the apostle Peter quoted in answering the inquiry of the crowd at Pentecost who wondered what was happening as they heard people speaking in languages they hadn't learned. He lifts his voice to the crowd and proclaims, "This is what was spoken by the prophet Joel," and he quotes the above passage in explaining a beautiful fact: What Moses hoped for and Joel foresaw was now beginning! The Holy Spirit had been outpoured, and now was present to fill every available person who would welcome His doing so. And with this fullness, He was not only coming to glorify Jesus Christ through each Christian, but He was also equipping each one with a potential for anointed speech.

Peter's application of Joel's prophecy contemporizes this promise for all time!

It is also significant to see how this first reference to all believers receiving the capability to prophesy is directly linked to the spiritual language. Notice that when Peter proclaims Joel's prophecy as being fulfilled, to that point the 120 worshipers had only spoken in tongues. However, the fact that some observers present had understood what they had said had already made these words prophetic. They were understood, and they stirred the hearts of the hearers. The supernatural glorifying of God Almighty had struck wonder in human souls. Thus, this first reference to all believers being potentially enabled to prophesy demonstrates the desirability of this capability enhancing each Christian's life. Here is the introduction of prophecy, but it is radically unlike and impossible to confuse with the occult enterprises that go under the same name.

Look at Acts 2 and see what happened:

- Christians were at prayer and were filled with the Holy Spirit (vv. 1–3).

- Overflowing in the Spirit, they speak with tongues, and some of these languages are understood by onlookers (vv. 4–10).

- Their words are heard and understood to be extolling God's wonderful works (v. 11).

- While some mock, a host of others are captivated and inquire to know more (vv. 12–13).

- As a result of this miraculous exercise—tongues-becoming-prophecy—God's Word is given by Peter, who answers their questions, and God's Son Jesus is exalted as Messiah and Lord (vv. 14–36).

- Three thousand individuals repent and are baptized; open to a life of faith in Christ Jesus through the same power of the Holy Spirit (vv. 37–41).

A Practice Worth Preserving

There is nothing but God's blessing and grace seen here—an order of blessing that helps us understand why the apostle Paul was so pointed and yet so patient with the Corinthian congregation. See his methodical dealing with prophecy as a practice worth preserving in the church's and the individual's experiences. He carefully teaches the difference between the spiritual language as a private and personal expression, as compared with its place as one means of introducing Holy-Spirit-prompted prophecies.

> I wish you all spoke with tongues, but even more that you prophesied; for he who prophesies is greater than he who speaks with tongues, unless indeed he interprets, that the church may receive edification.
>
> 1 Corinthians 14:5

Paul makes clear that prophesying may be either (1) by direct utterance in the language native to the hearers, or (2) by the joint exercise of the gift of tongues with the gift of interpretation. In short, if a message in tongues is interpreted to the understanding and edification of the hearers, it becomes "indeed" equivalent to a prophetic message.

It is this value that later occasions the apostle to write more lengthily, establishing ground rules intended to release the appropriate continuance of prophecy in its edifying power. Let's look at 1 Corinthians 14:23–32.

> Therefore if the whole church comes together in one place, and all speak with tongues, and there come in those who are uninformed or unbelievers, will they not say that you are out of your mind? But if all prophesy, and an unbeliever or an uninformed person comes in, he is convinced by all, he is judged by all. And thus the secrets of his heart are revealed; and so, falling down on his face, he will worship God and report that God is truly among you.
>
> How is it then, brethren? Whenever you come together, each of you has a psalm, has a teaching, has a tongue, has a revelation, has an interpretation. Let all things be done for edification. If anyone speaks in a tongue, let there be two or at the most three, each in turn, and let one interpret. But if there is no interpreter, let him keep silent in church, and let him speak to himself and to God. Let two or three prophets speak, and let the others judge. But if

anything is revealed to another who sits by, let the first keep silent. For you can all prophesy one by one, that all may learn and all may be encouraged. And the spirits of the prophets are subject to the prophets.

Now let's enumerate the clear, uncluttered, and forthright facts:

1. Spiritual language spoken without interpretation in the presence of unbelievers will cause confusion (v. 23).
2. But if all or any believers prophesy by the Holy Spirit, their words will penetrate the unbelievers' hearts (vv. 24–25).
3. Therefore, allow a place in your gatherings for the varied ministries of the Holy Spirit (v. 26).
4. Spiritual language should only be employed in the public gathering when it is interpreted, that the prophetic content may be understood and become edifying (vv. 27–28).
5. Although any number of believers present may prophesy in due course, it is best to exercise restraint and generally only have two or three do so at a gathering. Also, anything prophesied must remain subject to evaluation as to its truth or application (vv. 29–30).
6. All operations of the Holy Spirit are subject to Him for distribution (1 Cor. 12:11), but at the same time these are subject to the individual's own timing and method in exercising the delivery or ministering of the gift. In other words, no one should ever be allowed to indulge himself or herself and seek excuse by saying, "The Spirit came on me and I couldn't control myself" (vv. 31–32).

But How Does It Work Now?

I began by describing the first time I ever experienced and exercised the gift of prophecy. When that took place, I hardly understood any of the passage I have just cited, although I had been trained to allow for the possibility in our times of such ministries of the Holy Spirit. But when I was so simply and graciously ushered into the actual exercise of the gift of prophecy, I wasn't thinking of biblical guidelines or rules—I was simply responding to the Holy Spirit's presence. The fruit of what happened that night, as well as ongoingly in the lives of those who were ministered to in that moment, is suffi-cient to indicate I didn't violate anything.

But for most believers, the entrance into Holy Spirit operations is *not* a mechanical or academic matter. Teaching can be given, but proph-ecy doesn't spring up by one person's telling another, "Follow this handbook and this is what will happen." The manifestations of the Holy Spirit happen to people who hunger and thirst after God, people who want His ways to be realized in their life and who desire to see Jesus glorified. This isn't to suggest or recommend a casual or indifferent attitude toward the guidelines of the Bible on these subjects. But I want to emphasize that probably few if any of us will taste the fullness of the Spirit's broad and sweeping works of power if we are preoccupied with style or systems.

There is a style—it's God's love.

And there is a system—His grace.

But human mechanics don't produce prophecies; the Holy Spirit prompts and gives them. (He works where open hearts want to see God's love abound and where there is no confidence placed in the flesh or in the brain-or-brawn wisdom or power of man.)

So it is that I have described a deep "rumbling" up from my in-ner being when that first burst of prophecy rose in me. But it wasn't an incoherent or a mystical experience in the sense that I was trans-ported or lost control of my speech. What I saw was clear and simple: the blackness, the darkness, the horror of sin. And when I finally bel-lowed "Sin!" I didn't exclaim it in that fashion because I couldn't help it. I simply had to lift my voice because the awesome awfulness of what I saw made any other manner or method nondescriptive and inconsistent with the force of the "vision." Further, my directives is-sued to the people—"bow . . . come to the altar . . . pray"—were with authority, but they were not dictatorial. It was the power of God's presence that commandeered the moment. People did obey, but *not* because they were being manipulated, rather, because the most logical thing to do in the face of that moment of divine visita-tion was to act, and my simple directions gave a biblical, practical, and desirable course of action.

The reason I am holding my testimony up for scrutiny against the backdrop of Paul's instruction, and taking time to explain the various things that happened, is because of something I've learned. Through the years I've come to understand that the reason many Christians—even leaders—do not enter into the exercise of spiritual gifts is because they have certain reservations or preoccupations with what ultimately is a minutiae of matters which incline to halt their responding because of fears. But my hope is that these explanations, both of the text and the testimony I've related, might help you, the reader. No answer as to "How might the gift of prophecy operate in me?" can ever truly be complete. For we all are finally summoned to step out in childlike faith. But what is clearly essential for a start at responding or functioning in this ministry of the Spirit is this:

1. You must want the Holy Spirit to work through you. This isn't a matter of craving personal recognition or of prioritizing one gift above another. It is simply a matter of settling the issue for yourself; that as a believer, you are a potential candidate for experiencing a word of prophecy at some time or another. As Acts 2:17–18 declares it, the whole family of the redeemed are intended to share in this facet of ministry.

2. You would be wise not to attempt a handbook approach to this experience. The Holy Spirit has a way of preferring to catch us by surprise rather than by dealing with us through a calculated plan of our own. In that way He— not we—not only makes the choices of when, through whom, and to whom gifts may be delivered, but when it's over we are all the more conscious of how grace is the central feature of all these works of the Spirit.

The Grace in the Gifts

There is a fundamental reason that the core Greek word from which "charismatic" is derived (*charismata;* i.e., spiritual gifts) is *charis,* meaning "grace." Every aspect of our salvation in Jesus Christ is dependent upon God's grace, of that we hopefully have all been well schooled. Nonetheless, there tends to be a very subtle intrusion of human works which we Christians impose on the gifts. These tend to control or limit the possibilities of the Holy Spirit's working in the lives of many devoted believers. Often, more time is spent on reasoning and analyzing His works, or categorizing and assigning gifts to personality types, than is spent on simply calling us to abandon ourselves to them— indeed, to Him!

That the gifts of the Holy Spirit operate by grace is best understood if we remember this: Just as surely as the fact that none of us figures out how to be saved from sin, but we simply surrender ourselves through faith to the *finished work* of Jesus Christ, in the same way, the fullest working of the Holy Spirit becomes the portion of those who cease trying to figure out His gifts. The gifts of the Spirit flow where yielded vessels are willing to simply surrender themselves to His present workings. Oh, that we all might see the blessing of our God-given starting place in Christ and the beauty of our growing place in the Spirit!

- What the Lord Jesus has done to save us is finished—accomplished!
- What the Holy Spirit is doing to work through us is present—awaiting!

The common denominator to experiencing either—(1) salvation's foundation and forgiveness, or (2) the Spirit's fullness and ministry—is absolute dependence upon God and our surrendering to His terms. The fleshly mind may debate this proposition, but it's the only way for any of us to move into realizing the fuller potential of the Holy Spirit's workings in our hearts and through our lives.

There are reasons why the Holy Spirit offers us all the possibility of *both*—a capacity for experiencing spiritual language as well as a capability for exercising prophetic utterance:

- The first (spiritual language) has a way of humbling our pride; the second (prophetic utterance) prods us toward accepting our responsibility to give God's Word to others.
- The first enables broadened praise; the second enables broadened impact of our words.
- The first begets intercessory prayer; the second begets insightful speech both in public and private.

In the light of this biblically established availability of spiritual resources for us all, let's take a closer look at how prophecy happens to people.

Learning about Prophesying

First, a speaker may be said to be prophesying when a divine anointing is upon what he or she is saying. This is not at all always spontaneous, but very often relates to something spoken which has been prepared in advance. In such instances, the prophetic anointing:

1. began with the presence of the Holy Spirit in the Scriptures they studied in preparation;
2. became alive to them as they prayerfully prepared and were filled with a passion for God's will to be done—feeling compassion for those to whom they would speak; then the anointing
3. became manifest during the delivery of the message.

We have all frequently seen this kind of prophecy. It is usually manifested through such noted evangelists as Billy Graham, James Robison, Reinhard Bonnke, Luis Palau, and others of similar renown. But it also manifests thousands of times every week through pastors and teachers who deliver their messages and lessons with a distinct quality of the Holy Spirit's presence being sensed by those hearing them. This order of prophecy ought not be presumed or overlooked. It isn't prophecy because it's spoken, but because it's anointed. And it isn't better because it's presented by apparently better qualified people. God delights to speak through all His own; which leads to the second facet of prophecy—a functional manifestation of the Holy Spirit which may be realized by either a platformed or an unplatformed believer.

A *second* and less recognized ministry of the Holy Spirit in prophesying occurs when a Christian either hears, sees, or senses a prompting from the Holy Spirit and speaks what he or she has received. These three verbs—hear, see, sense—are important to helping most Christians come to recognize how the Holy Spirit may give them a word of prophecy, a gift to be delivered to someone needing the ministry that gift will supply.

God has created each of us with uniqueness that often is manifested in the different ways we perceive things. Some people describe God's dealing with them as a voice; another as, "I saw something"; and others, "I felt or sensed an impression." Because the prompting of the Holy Spirit is unique with each of the Lord's people (though general categories are discernible) there is sometimes unnecessary confusion or fruitless debate surrounding terms. Or if no argument over terms occurs (for example, "What does he mean, 'God spoke to me'?!"), there is still a tendency for you or me to expect that our experience should or will be the same as someone else's testimony.

The "hearing" that people describe is not the same as the psychological or spiritual problem of someone who "hears voices." There is a world of difference between voices and the Voice. Jesus said, "My sheep know my voice," and it can be said with certainty that when the Lord speaks to you or me there will be a confidence it is Him speaking. The reasons are simple:

1. The Lord never says anything contrary to His Word.
2. The Lord never says anything unfilled with love.
3. The Lord never says anything uncontributive to peace.

This is what the Scripture means when it says, "He who prophesies speaks edification, exhortation, and comfort to men" (1 Cor. 14:3). In other words, prophecy always builds up (edification), stirs up (exhortation) or lifts up (comfort). Prophecy never condemns, never seeks to dominate or control the direction of another person's life, and it never removes the focus of the message from Christ to the person who is prophesying.

In the same way, things "seen" by the Spirit does not mean a person is in a trance or lost to a present consciousness of other things around them. I saw the churning blackness, and sensed it was a picture of sin. Such vision is not a claim to equality with John's experience on Patmos, but it is one of the very real ways prophecies are given by the Holy Spirit to our understanding.

At yet other times, a mental impulse—words, thoughts, a memorized verse, a Bible reference to turn to—are impressions the Holy Spirit uses to prompt prophecy. Thus we might identify His dealings with any one of us.

But Why Would Anyone Want to Prophesy?

The foremost reason for seeking to disengage this beautiful manifestation of the Holy Spirit from the excess baggage, superstition, and fear that have often attended it is because of the immensely profitable benefit it can be when freely, wisely, and tenderly ministered.

That first of mine, so many years ago when God unveiled to my vision the awfulness of sin in its blinding, binding ways, opened the doorway to a response pattern I gradually learned to exercise. While a word of prophecy would only come to me once in a while early in my learning to respond, there were still remarkable things that happened. I've come to realize that these were not uncommon things, in the sense that I know thousands of Christians—leaders and laity alike—who have gradually come to function with regularity in such simply beautiful operations of the Holy Spirit. The value and blessing of such ministry is very real.

For example, I remember Pat's sitting in my office, seeking help for a problem. As I spoke with her, I felt quite keenly that her problem wasn't the matter she was discussing, but rather was rooted to a hidden fear in her soul. As we talked, one sentence continued to forcibly and recurrently come to my mind. I finally decided it was the Holy Spirit giving me a word of prophecy.

"Pat," I said, "I want you to know that I feel very deeply about the concern you have over . . ." (and I mentioned the problem she was describing).

"But," I continued, "I want to ask you a question—and I ask your patience for interrupting what we've been talking about." She said, "That's okay," and invited me to go ahead.

As I began to speak the following sentence, I felt a sudden surge of compassion, as though I were speaking to her personally, bringing a message our loving Lord felt very desirous of giving to her.

"Pat, I feel the Lord Himself wants me to speak these words to you in His behalf. He's saying, 'I will never cause the shame of your nakedness to appear.'" (Those were the exact words I had been hearing or sensing recurrently over the preceding many minutes.)

The impact was electric.

She instantly began to weep, almost uncontrollably. After a minute or two she regained her composure and began to explain.

"Pastor, I don't know how to describe this, but those words spoke directly to the deepest fear I've had. For the longest time, the exact words, 'I'll be left naked and ashamed,' would repeatedly express themselves to my mind. I've felt that someday I'll be left alone with nothing, as though life would suddenly turn into a bad dream and I would be naked before a crowd of people, embarrassed, and mocked. But when you said—I mean, when the Lord gave you those words, I *know* it was the Lord! Only He could know the words that have been in my mind and the fear that has been at the bottom of my other problems. That was the heart of them all: I feared I would end up alone, uncovered, uncared for, and ashamed."

There are other times when a word of prophecy is for public declaration.

Recently, following an extended season of intercession for the breaking of a drought in our congregation's part of our nation, one of our pastoral staff stood and prophesied a dual outpouring. "The rain shall come in both the natural and the spiritual realm; there will be the blessing of rain upon your land and a season of blessing of the Spirit poured out in your midst." The prophecy specifically emphasized—it was repeated three times—"I will send the rains with thunders of my power."

In most parts of the United States, thunder and rain are commonly joined, but in Southern California, thunderstorms are very rare. Still, beginning the very next week—after an extensive drought—mighty deluges of rain poured over the entire region, as unusual thunderclaps with lightning shook the area. And even further and more blessed, the dual outpouring occurred in the spiritual realm as well as in the natural, for during the following weeks several hundred souls came to Christ as God moved in might and grace among us in the church.

There are seemingly infinite illustrations possible, but the reason for simply relating these two is to note the relative desirability of individuals and congregations welcoming this operation of God's grace into their ongoing experience. It *is* a part of the beauty of spiritual language, because so frequently prophecy comes by tongues and interpretation, even though the supernatural language is not always present.

But What about the Crazies?

It's risky to use the word "crazies." There *are* aberrant exercises at times and there *are* peculiar people. I mean strange people who either claim to bring prophecies (or who actually *do*), doing so in ways that render them suspect of less than wisdom or sound-mindedness. The list of strange things trails from prophecies of tragedy or destruction, or of the Second Coming of Christ (all on a specific date), to prophecies directing who a certain person is to marry (or break up with, or divorce, or who knows what else), or, "Joe and Cecile should move to Tennessee!" (and they do and lose their shirts). The horror stories have a way of multiplying and being embellished. Often, anyone opposing the true contemporary manifestations of the Holy Spirit will present the crazies or the horror stories as the standard or the mocked stereotype example of prophesying. But in reality, the reason such happenings find any place at all is because there is such a general ignorance of the true exercise of the Spirit's working in prophesying.

The solution is not to despise prophesying, for the Bible expressly prohibits that (1 Thess. 5:20). But to obey that command successfully, prophecies need to be permitted, to be welcomed, understood, and applied. Still, in exercising this openness, what none of us need to do is accept everything that is prophesied or simply any way a prophecy may be expressed. Just because someone says, "Thus saith the Lord," doesn't mean that God necessarily "saith-ed" anything whatsoever. Or if Wild-eyed Willie sidles toward the microphone whispering, "I believe I have a word from the Lord," it's likely that most everybody already knows that Willie gets strange ideas and blames God for them. So you don't need to let Willie loose again, as though you were despising prophecies if you didn't. Willie just might have a genuine word of prophecy some day, but he's as responsible as anyone else to establish credibility by a sensible pattern of behavior before anyone is obligated to listen up.

Claiming divine prompting is never a substitute for a sound-minded, trust-begetting, Christ-like lifestyle. More genuine workings of the Holy Spirit have been removed from consideration due to just plain goofiness than ever by outright error. The crazies are alive, but unfortunately they're not well. When we decide we don't have to open up to nonsense because we open up to the supernatural, the supernatural will become a good deal more natural; that is, "natural" in terms of its frequency and its comforting, God-blessed beauty in our midst.

Be assured that:

- Prophecies don't have to be delivered unnaturally, loudly, or in Shakespearian English. Volume isn't wrong, for sometimes the message has an urgency that recommends proclamation. But a shriek or a shrillness isn't essential to demonstrate anointing. The language form may be common, but voices needn't quaver. In other words, the Holy Ghost doesn't mean to make us ghostly.

- Prophecies don't have to be surrendered to. That is, the leader of the meeting doesn't need to redirect anything just because something was said. It's not unusual for a sincere but insensitive soul to bring a word that has no bearing on what is in progress in the meeting. The leader's kind remark, "To whomever that may speak, God bless you," and then a quick progressing on with the service, can turn the corner. (If anyone has a habit of ill-timed words, he or she should be spoken to in private by the elders and assisted to think more clearly about the propriety of what he or she has to bring before bringing it.)

- Prophecies may be corrected. If there is something clearly erroneous, correct it. And if it is unclear, ask the persons bringing the word to clarify it. If they say they don't know what they mean, then a later contact to clarify their own thinking about prophesying may be necessary. On occasion, if a word seemed erratic, judgmental, or bizarre, I have simply asked openly of elders and deacons present, "Who of you confirm this word?" In such obvious cases, there are usually none whatsoever. Thus, much to the congregation's comfort, the situation is immediately addressed and it is made evident again that our openness to the supernatural has not surrendered us to the stupid or the superstitious. (Incidentally, the few times the above has happened, the persons bringing the word have always been visitors. I can almost assure any congregation seeking to open their worship to a place for the prophetic that such visitors will appear. I sometimes think they're beamed down from somewhere in outer space, but even if that's not true, I can tell you for sure they're from somewhere in deep left field!)

Then, too, there are specific positives we should expect of words from the Lord; that is, genuine operations of the Holy Spirit giving prophecies to people for delivery to the body of the church or to smaller groups.

First, they will somehow draw us toward a basic biblical truth. Prophecies are in no wise and never to be equated with the Scriptures, but they should have both their root and their fruit there. I mean, a word, however it may be expressed, should be centered in a concept that is recognizably biblical. This doesn't mean it needs to quote Scripture, and a prophecy doesn't require an exposition of a text or a detailed teaching. But vital words do have a way of making something we've already known in the Word become fresh to our understanding and vital to our perspective for this moment.

I was at a pastor's conference when a word was given: "I am speaking to all of you as shepherds of My flock, and I speak to you as your Great Shepherd of the sheep, your Lord and Master. I call you to humility, remembering that before I became known as the Great Shepherd, I first became the Lamb of God. Remember that, and lay your life down in service to your flock. Only as you learn my heart as the Lamb will you understand my heart as a Shepherd." The response was one of brokenness and humbling. No new truth had been spoken, but a perspective on principles clearly in the Scriptures took on a focus and force that was inescapable.

Second, let us positively minister words of prophecy with sobriety, sensitivity, and a spiritual bearing. It is not becoming that a person claiming to prophesy simply ramble on, or stare about the room, or smile into a television camera, or chat in a folksy manner, or seize the meeting without regard for those in leadership. Any of those things are unbecoming and are understandably objectionable. Instead, let us:

1. Ascertain the acceptability of a word as to its time in the service. (Even as the senior pastor of our congregation, if I have a prophecy and I am not leading the meeting at the moment, I notify the leader and wait until he or she acknowledges the right time.)

2. Keep the prophecy as brief as possible. People cannot follow the thought of a wandering word. A word is exactly that—a clear, distinct idea; clearly spoken and concisely related. It usually is built around a picture of some kind; for example, a river running to the sea, a cloud drawing near with rain, a tree with fruit of mixed quality, etc. These figures are actual ones from the Bible (which isn't a requirement), but they do illustrate that prophecy very often has an element of poetic imagery to it that helps the hearer see what the Lord is saying.

Third, help the people focus on the Lord, in whose Name the word is being brought. It doesn't seem appropriate to deliver a word to a watching crowd, save in rare occasions where the mantle of a prophet is upon the preacher as he addresses the congregation. Even if the spokesperson's eyes are opened, it helps the people focus on the content rather than the speaker if they are invited, thus: "Let's all simply bow our heads a moment and receive this word one of the brothers/sisters has for us."

How Is Prophesying Kept in Perspective?

Like any operation of God's gracious purposes, exaggerated emphasis is always a potential plague.

I was dismayed a few years ago when a movement I respect suddenly seemed taken in by a passion for prophets and prophesying. Thankfully, the fascination was relatively brief, but not without a certain amount of difficulty and distraction (if not destruction) taking place. When imbalance occurs with regard to any aspect of the spiritual gifts, there is a rush in two directions. The first is a rush against the particular manifestation, usually led by those who deny the presence of spiritual gifts as biblically acceptable today. The second is a rush from the exercise of whatever gifts or manifestations are involved. Sometimes, many remove themselves from practicing what they actually believe can be presently expected, but who now avoid a valid practice for fear of guilt by association with those involved in extreme or aberrant applications of the gifts.

A number of seasoned leaders have grappled with these problems, and there are good guidelines which we can apply to the practice of the gift of prophecy. And in doing so, may we experience the joy, profit, and vitality of keeping open to what the Spirit is saying to the church. Let us remember:

1. God's Word must always be elevated as the plumb line by which all prophetic utterance is measured.

2. God's Word, the Bible, must always be the focus of our hunger for truth, growth in faith, and guidance for life.

3. Jesus Christ Himself must always be the center of focus; no gift or its exercise drawing us from Him to focusing on a human instrument.

4. All exercise of gifts in a congregation must be in submission

to local church eldership, not as a controlling device but as a means of protection, adjustment, and correction.

5. All prophecy should be applied, not merely applauded. The word of the Holy Spirit is to call us to action, not to entertain or excite us.

6. Personal prophecies should never introduce control or direction over human beings. Christ, not prophets or prophecies, is the Lord of each of His redeemed.

7. Always remember, "We prophesy in part," and therefore no prophesy is a final word on something, nor necessarily to be received as a timeless direction on anything.

With the sad tales of prophecies *mis*handled unto destructiveness, there are seemingly as many humorous stories of prophecies *man*-handled unto ridiculousness.

A friend of mine was visiting England and heard of a house meeting where a diligent soul rose to speak. The young man who rose apparently intended to quote a historic saint as a part of his opening words—but it came out like this: "Thus says the Lord: 'As I said by my servant (pause) I think it was John Wesley, but I'm not sure . . .'" Although he continued, his listeners had a hard time repressing laughter, since the fumbling of the speaker had seemed to attribute a sag in the memory of the Almighty.

Another classic comes from the Deep South, where a shrill voice proclaimed from the rear of the church one Sunday: "The Lord says, 'There's fear in the East, there's fear in the West, and I'm kinda skeered Myself!'"

These true stories are certainly evidence that God has made Himself incredibly vulnerable by opening the door to His own and offering His Spirit to prompt them with words of prophecy. Apparently in His open-handed readiness to distribute gifts of grace to mankind at the broadest dimensions, He's willing to run the risk of human blunderings. To multiply His avenues of outpouring, He has chosen to enfranchise as many as possible, saying, "Upon all my sons and daughters"; a word from His changeless Word—the Holy Bible. The Holy Spirit wants to use you to edify, exhort, and comfort others, and He will increase your understanding of how that may increase in your personal life and ministry if you'll allow Him. Never be distracted by the detractors. Spirit-filled living was always intended to include this practice—this expectation.

One man shouts, "To claim to hear from God or to claim to speak a word in His Name is to deny the absolute finality of the Scriptures or to manifest your sense of their insufficiency."

Ridiculous! Worse yet, it's unscriptural itself, however strong its claim to be defending the inspiration of God's timeless, eternal Word. God *does* speak to His own, and He *does* illumine insights to their minds—insights which are alive with present urgency and which will always keep our focus on Christ and the Bible.

As to such ludicrous accusations: I've never yet met a thinking saint who heard a word of prophecy and would even remotely consider ripping his Bible open and adding the prophetic word just spoken to the pages of the Scriptures. Nor do I know anyone of even the slightest understanding of Spirit-filled living who dotes over prophecies at the expense of searching and feeding on the pure milk and solid meat of the Word of God.

God *is* speaking by His Spirit to hosts of people today. And more and more are listening—unto their edification, exhortation, and comfort. And among the ones I observe, the most satisfying thing is that the more they listen to what the Spirit is saying, the more they love and live like what He has conclusively said in the Book—His Holy Word.

8

A Beauty with Blessed Benefits

As Charles Dickens has Tiny Tim say in the conclusion to *A Christmas Carol:* "God bless us . . . every one!"

*I*t was another Christmastime at the Hayford household and I was feeling rather smug about my gift plans for Anna. She has outplanned me so many times, surprising me with things I hadn't imagined as she thoughtfully prepared all year long for what she would give me. But this time I was sure I was about to top her—and my love for this dear lady with whom I've spent decades of marriage joy made it especially fulfilling to anticipate.

I'd prepared one of those big-boxes-with-lots-of-little-boxes-inside kind of presents. And when Christmas Eve arrived, all of us—the kids, grandkids, and of course me (Grampa/Dad/Hubby)—laughed, clapped and cried as Anna (Gramma/Mom/Sweetheart-wife) opened each individual present within the larger box.

Our boys had hoisted the big box in front of their mother, and all eyes turned to watch—I saw to that: "Hey kids, it's time to watch your Dad shine. Come 'round and see what I got your Mom!" There were practical gifts, beautiful gifts, clothing gifts, and sentimental gifts. (There were tears when Anna opened a portrait of her mother I had had framed—a touching picture of a pioneer-spirited woman, now ninety-two years old, who raised nine children on the Nebraska plains).

That scene comes to mind as an apt picture of the Heavenly Father's heart toward the Bride of Christ. It's appropriate because, in fact, every good and perfect gift comes from Him (James 1:17), and each of the multitudinous mercies, goodnesses, abundances, and gifting He lavishes are bound up in one great package—the gift of eternal

life. That grand, all-inclusive gift, with all that potentially will be discovered within it, was purchased through the One whose Blood paid
for such lovingkindness to be poured out upon us—our Lord, Jesus
Christ, the Father's Son.

In reality, the whole of salvation is wrapped in one large package:
Jesus. So from the inception of our new life in Christ we have the full
bounty of all that is promised us. But just as my wife needed to unwrap
each of the individual gifts within the larger giftbox, it is similarly true
that each of us is called to partake, to decisively open and receive to
ourselves each of the many blessings, provisions, and gifts God has for
us.

There is a theological accuracy in the proposition that everything
we receive from God is delivered to us when we receive Jesus as Savior
and Lord. But equally important, there is a practical necessity. The application of each facet of God's resource for our lives depends upon
our unwrapping what He's provided. You and I need to take, receive,
and open each portion within the promise—taking it unto ourselves,
opening to the possibilities inherent in each part of the full dimensions
of life we've been given through Jesus Christ.

The resource of the spiritual language is among these packages in
Christ. As we've earlier noted, speaking with tongues is as available to
each Christian as to any other. When Peter said, "Repent, be baptized
and you shall receive the gift of the Holy Spirit," he announced the
availability of an enormous package including innumerable blessings,
invested with eternal power, and inviting expanding participation.

The marvel of God's individual gifts, however, is that the smaller
presents within the greater are each laden with His creativity and spiritual wealth. Thus, to open any single package is to discover yet again
another whole realm of unfolding gifts and graces. Just as one of my
Christmas gifts to Anna was a pearl necklace, so God will unveil one
gift within *the* Gift to reveal a string of individual treasures within any
single one of His many love-gifts to us. The beauty of spiritual language is like this.

That there are many varied benefits in the spiritual language is
outlined by Paul in his 1 Corinthians 14 corrective instruction on its
use. It is his recognition of these values within the gift of the language
itself that is doubtless at the root of his being so affirming about
tongues: "I would you all spoke with tongues. . . . I speak with
tongues more than you all. . . . Do not forbid to speak with tongues"
(vv. 5, 18, 39).

His stern instruction is pointed: "Don't abuse sane public exercise" (vv. 11, 23); "Don't go public without interpretation" (v. 28); "Don't say, 'I couldn't control myself'—because you can!" (v. 32). Such direct and demanding controls are for an even greater reason than the obvious goal of avoiding confusion and disorder in the assembly's gatherings. Beyond this, the apostle is seeking to also establish sound policies of practice which will assure that the *personal* benefits inherent within the private, devotional exercise of the spiritual language are preserved.

There are at least three blessed additional benefits in an ongoing private use of spiritual language; that is, three in addition to the two we've discussed earlier—expanded worship and enabled warfare. Along with the resource of praying with tongues to bring a fresh fragrance to worship and a holy firepower to our intercessory warfare, the spiritual language may be unwrapped to discover even more inside this gift within the Gift. First Corinthians 14, as well as correcting abuse, points to our enlightened use of the spiritual language as:

1. A means for edifying the soul (v. 4a).
2. A means for distinct communication (v. 2a).
3. A means for solving "mysteries" (v. 2b).

Each of these applications awaits the employment of the believer. None of them occur by some magical means or by a holy seizure. God never deals with His redeemed in occult or other ways which bypass our choice to participate in His provisions. So it's more than appropriate—it's desirable to look into these biblically revealed possibilities. To do so is to see how they expressly fulfill Jesus' prophecy about the infilling of the Holy Spirit.

Rivers He Promised

In John 7, the Lord was at the Feast of Tabernacles. On that occasion just six months before He would be crucified, He made an announcement to the huge crowd gathered for the feast's climactic moment. The water-pouring ceremony—commemorating the miraculous supply of water God gave Israel during its wilderness journey—was just now taking place. As the priests tipped giant basins of water, which go splashing down the temple steps, John told what happened:

On the last day, that great day of the feast, Jesus stood and cried out, saying, "If anyone thirsts, let him come to Me and drink. He who believes in Me, as the Scripture has said, out of his heart will flow rivers of living water." But this He spoke concerning the Spirit, whom those believing in Him would receive; for the Holy Spirit was not yet given, because Jesus was not yet glorified.

John 7:37–39

Please notice the plural term—"rivers"—which our Savior prophesies, detailing the nature of the inner resource which would become available to those who would later receive the fullness of the Holy Spirit. "Rivers" are a distinct contrast to the "well" imagery Jesus uses in John 4, where He speaks to the woman needing salvation's promise of eternal life, forgiveness of sin, and the hope of future glory. He told her, "If you knew the gift of God . . . you would ask and He would give you living water . . . for the water that I will give becomes a fountain, welling up into everlasting life" (John 4:10, 14).

But here, of us who already believe, He describes cascading rivers as distinct from soul-saving wells. The contrast between rivers which flow from a person, and wells which rise within a person is not an accident of figurative speech. Jesus is describing things that occur within the believer's experience; things which are each designed by God's creative wisdom to accomplish different works. The well of eternal life answers to our soul's need for life unto salvation; the rivers of Holy Spirit workings answer to our personal need to be fully resourced for conveying the ministry Christ wants to work through each of us to touch the world around us. The well brings eternal life, the rivers surge with holy power; the well is for our salvation, the rivers are for our life of service.

As we examine the Word of God, investigating the dynamic uses of the spiritual language in our daily life, allow me to employ Jesus' figure of rivers to illustrate three blessed benefits.

The River of Edification

He who speaks in a tongue edifies himself . . .

1 Corinthians 14:4

But you, beloved, building yourselves up on your most holy faith, praying in the Holy Spirit, keep yourselves in the love of God, looking for the mercy of our Lord Jesus Christ unto eternal life.

Jude 20–21

The sands of the Sahara spread before my gaze as the blistering heat rose in shimmering waves to the west. I was standing on a ridge hardly twenty miles from downtown Cairo when, as I simply turned 180 degrees from my westward view toward the east and the city, I was riveted with the stark differences. Egypt's most populated area lay before me, bustling with life. The verdant greenery was everywhere and glistened like emeralds on the shores of the Nile which stretched off to both the south and north. I was in awe of the startling difference. From the ridge, looking eastward: life, wealth, fruitfulness, and beauty—everywhere. To the west, virtually nothing. It all changed so rapidly—as though a line were drawn in the sand: businesses and buildings to the east, including the wonders of the Great Pyramids; barrenness and boiling sand to the west, the only wonder being in the question—How long could anyone last out there?

If I ever saw a sight that interpreted the power of a river to edify—to build up—it was there. The dramatic impression and illustration have lived with me since that day.

The concept of edification is simplest to explain when we remember that a building is often referred to as an edifice. The Bible describes three means for the building up of a Christian's life.

1. We are being built up as a spiritual house, by the will and the hand of Christ Himself. "I will build My Church . . ." (Matt. 16:18); "the whole building being joined together grows into a holy temple unto the Lord" (Eph. 2:21); and, "You also, as living stones, are being built up a spiritual house . . ." (1 Pet. 2:25). In this respect, we are subjects of a divinely ordained building project, each one being tooled by God's hand to fit us together as parts of a house called the household of faith.

2. We are called to build each other up as mutual strengtheners of one another. "Excel to the edifying of the church" (1 Cor. 14:12, 5, 26); "Let us pursue . . . the things by which one may edify another" (Rom. 14:19); and "The whole body joined . . . causes growth of the body for the edifying of itself in love" (Eph. 4:16). In this respect, we are servants of one another, called to do everything possible to ensure the upward development and settled strength of each other as fellow servants of our Lord Jesus Christ.

3. We are directed to build up ourselves by a specific plan of Holy-Spirit-enabled prayer. "You, beloved, build up yourselves . . . praying in the Holy Spirit" (Jude 20); "He that prays in a tongue edifies himself" (1 Cor. 14:4). In comparison with the first two roles we fill as subjects and as servants in the edifying process, in this third respect we are stimulators of our own edification. These texts on edifying ourselves do *not* say we accomplish the building by our power. However, we *are* the ones who choose to employ the spiritual language—a God-appointed means for edifying our souls. The power is His as the Holy Spirit flows through and over our being with a river of edification, but the choice is ours: building up ourselves.

It's important to point out that this self-edification is not a selfish action; it's a scriptural one. It's a beautiful benefit of the spiritual language which I have drawn upon time and again.

I remember a season sometime back involving an overwhelmingly strenuous schedule. One evening during this time, I stood among the worshipers in a church service where I was to speak. I felt bone weary and mentally numb, stressed by the demands of duty. As I tried to consciously measure what I thought my physical and spiritual resources were for the message I was to bring, I nearly wept. And it was there, as I felt such a desperate weakness, that the Holy Spirit brought to mind the text above. I was prompted by God's Word to draw by faith upon the potential within the spiritual language to edify myself. So, while the congregation was singing, I stood unobtrusively in the front row of the sanctuary, my back toward the congregation so no one could see my lips. Then, as they sang, as an act of my own will, I took the entirety of the time worshiping with my spiritual language.

To anyone else I would only have appeared to be singing with the congregation. But minute by minute, as I sang with the spirit, I became conscious of a steady increase of strength and refreshing within my whole being. My physical frame, my mental mind-set, and my spiritual preparedness were all refurbished marvelously. My sudden transformation was characterized by what one might expect of the fulfillment of Isaiah 28, the same prophetic context from which Paul quotes regarding spiritual language in 1 Corinthians 14:21: "'This is the rest with which you may cause the weary to rest,' and 'This is the refreshing'" (see Isa. 28:12).[1]

Self-edification is also available when we're conscious of something more than weariness:

- It's an intended resource when I know a difficult situation is coming up;
- It's a refreshing in the midst of spiritual warfare;
- It's a means of imbibing strength when facing temptation, or a means of inviting God's wisdom when needing to make a decision.

Joined alongside of (1) fellowship with other Christians and (2) feeding on the Word of God, (3) the river of edification is a stream of Holy-Spirit-enabled language which has been provided to us as a distinct benefit. But like all benefits available under any contract or relationship, they need to be applied for. God has provided this for us: It's our choice to draw upon and utilize it.

The River of Communication

He who speaks in a tongue does not speak to men but to God.

1 Corinthians 14:2

For if I pray in a tongue, my spirit prays, but my understanding is unfruitful.

1 Corinthians 14:14

The most fundamental insight 1 Corinthians 14 provides is that the spiritual language is a multi-purpose resource. Any definition of speaking with tongues that confines the practice to one purpose will only bring confusion about the blessing of the spiritual language. Just as certainly as the subject is confused if the grace of the spiritual language is not distinguished from the gift (see chapter 6), so must we gain focus on the spectrum of applied purposes of these rivers of supernatural resource.

It was wintertime on the Mississippi, but the brilliance of the morning sun brightening the February day was not able to warm it much. Driving from Moline to Davenport, Anna and I pulled onto a viewpoint which the river-spanning bridge allowed midway across the "Mighty Miss'." Though jacketed against the chilling winds, our faces were unguarded and our viewing time was voluntarily shortened as we hurried back to the shelter of our car, but not before I had noticed an item of interest.

Although the river was completely frozen over, toward the western bank a channel had been cut in the ice to allow the flow of boat traffic, a flow which is so essential to the economy of the region. I'm not informed of what demands for maintenance such a wintertime channel requires to keep the ice pack back and retain an open concourse, but the visual message fixed itself in my memory.

Do you have winter seasons of your soul? Of course, we all do! To mind come the number of times my situation has been snowed in or frozen over by sudden or accumulated pressures or trials. Do you understand exactly what I mean when I confess, "Sometimes I don't feel like praying at all, and other times, though I do pray, it seems like nothing is happening—nothing but *nothing*"? The psalmists and the prophets made the same confession on occasions. Their candor comforts us, but it also invites us to lay aside religious pretension and "tell it like it seems" sometimes. In these wintertimes of the soul, you or I may seem to need a jump start, for many are the times it's hard to pray. The mind wanders and the chill seems almost to have closed the windows of heaven.

But the apostle Paul writes of a sure-fire connection between two spirits, between the redeemed human spirit and the Living Father, our Eternal Creator Himself. An assurance is wrapped in the words of the text above: When words fail and the soul seems chilled, there's a hot line to heaven that goes directly to the throne, a channel of holy commerce that never freezes, over whatever the conditions on our side of things! Let's allow the Holy Spirit to assist us in praying beyond our sensed limits of such moments. The simple statement of the Word is this: When I pray in tongues, I'm talking to God. Period! Whatever else anyone may say about the employment of spiritual language, this is the Bible's bottom line. Tongues are connected to heaven's throne; that's all there is to it.

Of course, this is not to demean the validity of prayer in our native language as though it were second class. But however efficient my "prayer with my understanding," even at best there are two limits which recommend my supplementing all "prayer with my understanding" with prayers "in the Spirit." First, no matter how much I may understand about that for which I pray, I probably never understand everything. Praying in the

Spirit expands beyond those limitations. Second, whenever my feelings of frozenness or my absence of spiritual zeal block my mind for prayer, my spirit can still find a release that will break the ice and open the channels by the Holy Spirit's assistance.

These facts might lead someone to suggest that if spiritual language prayer is so effective, then why not *only* pray with the Spirit? The answer is that the Bible teaches otherwise. The enablement of spiritual language is not an argument for mental sloth or intellectual laziness. God's formula is clearly stated in His Word; "I will pray with the spirit, *and* I will also pray with the understanding" (1 Cor. 14:15), so I am wise to utilize both resources—my native language, "with understanding," and my spiritual language, "with the spirit."

In this same regard, let me address another matter; a problem that may be one of the most common distractions faced by people who open themselves to the practice of spiritual language by the Holy Spirit's power. The challenge comes in the form of questions that will occasionally badger the mind, like:

How do I know this is really a language?

Is this really doing any good?

Why are the words I speak so often repeated?

I've taken comfort first and foremost in the fact that I've never known of any God-given experience or resource that the adversary of our souls won't challenge with similar doubts. "How do you know you're really saved?" "Why do you believe this Book is the Word of God?" "What difference do you think getting wet (baptism) will make, anyway?" "Don't you think it's silly to go through the motions with that bread and wine?" "C'mon, you don't really need to go to church—you can worship right here at home!"

Both our flesh and the devil will challenge fundamental disciplines of spiritual life and seek to erode convictions in an effort to gain our surrender of their potential vitality for our life. But the Bible's words on the privileged discipline of employing spiritual language give both an assurance and an answer: "The one who speaks with tongues *is* speaking to God!" Let this assurance buttress your mind against doubt. God's Word says, "Believe this—you're speaking to Me, and I am hearing and will respond to everything your heart is expressing by my Spirit." And the next time the adversary whispers: "It doesn't sound like a language to me," use 1 Corinthians 14:2 for your text and reply: "That's because I wasn't talking to you!"

Some years ago I learned to apply to this subject one of the New Testament's basic principles: "Ask, and it will be given unto you"; and "For whoever has, to him more will be given" (Matt. 7:7; 13:12). The principle is that God will give what we request, and when we use what He gives He will multiply it. It's a simple point of wisdom to apply this promise in answer to any question rising in your mind due to an apparently limited vocabulary in your spiritual language.

My daughter, Christa, and I were talking together one day during her early teenage years. Since praying with the spirit was normal in our family, it was quite a natural thing that she asked me, "Dad, could you help me? Sometimes I doubt my spiritual language because it sounds like I often am saying the same words over and over."

"I know what you mean, Hon," I assured her. "I think all of us have had that experience." She looked surprised. (Isn't it strange how many of us tend to think we're the only ones who have ever had a particular problem!)

"Let me share two things with you, Chris," I continued. "First, I want to ask you a question. If all I was ever able to say to you were the words, 'I love you,' and you knew I really meant them even though I couldn't say anything else, would you think that was bad?"

"No," she expressed understandingly.

"Well, from what we *do* know about what our spiritual language means, it's certainly something very, very good and praiseful to the Father." (I explained Acts 2:11 and our text here, 1 Cor. 14:2, then went on.) "Since we're 'talking to God' directly, and if we mean what we pray with our whole heart—just like if I really meant 'I love you'—can you imagine God saying, 'I don't like what you're saying, because it's too few words and you keep repeating yourself?'"

She laughed. "No, Dad," and smiling she continued, "I get the point. I just need to believe the Bible and *know* that He receives what I'm saying as really 'loving' to Him."

"You got it," I said. "But one thing more. Do you remember Jesus' saying, 'He that is faithful in a few things I will make a ruler over many'?" (Matt. 25:23).

She said she did.

"Well, let me suggest something, since Jesus is the One who said that. Sometime in the next few days, while you're talking with the Lord, simply say: 'Lord Jesus, I thank You for the love language of worship

You've given me by the Holy Spirit, and I have tried to be faithful in using it. But I would like to speak even more in my spiritual language than I do now. So I'm simply asking if You would expand my language in the next little while.'"

We concluded our conversation with a few other thoughts, and I left the matter with her, knowing she was sincere and believing she'd do better making the application of our conversation on her own rather than my pressing the point right then.

About two weeks later Christa was walking through the living room where I was reading. She stopped and came over beside me.

"Hey, Dad. Just a quick minute. Seeing you reading there reminded me of our talk about spiritual language the other day—about, you know, asking Jesus to expand my language? Remember?"

"Sure, Honey. I remember."

"Well," she said, almost matter of factly, with a sweet smile, "I just wanted to tell you—I did and He did! Isn't that neat!"

And I hugged her and just said, "Yeah, Honey. It's really neat." And with that, a naturally supernatural, just-plain teenager who regularly talks with the Creator of the universe in more languages than she's ever learned (but ones He always understands) skipped on into the kitchen to dry the dishes.

The River of Unveiled Mysteries

> He who speaks in a tongue . . . in the spirit he speaks mysteries.
> 1 Corinthians 14:2

The word "mystery" has become altogether more mysterious in our day than it was in Bible times. Today "mystery" refers to the inscrutable, the unknown, or that which only a steel-trap, Sherlock-Holmes-type mind can demystify and master. And the plural "mysteries" is even worse, having come to bespeak the rites of an ancient religion or the arcane insights of an occult school of practice—perhaps on the order of reading tea leaves or divining a calf's liver!

But in the New Testament Greek the word "mystery" (*musterion*) means something almost the opposite: "a former secret now disclosed or opened." The only thing mysterious in the real definition is possibly that something had been a secret, but in the New Testament this word was used after the secret was shown, opened, known to all parties involved: nothing mysterious about it! But centuries of use do strange things to words, and the demystifying of "mystery" is important. We want to understand how the Holy Spirit enables us to speak mysteries, to, as it were, "speak former secrets into the light" as we pray in our spiritual language. So to do this, we need to go back to the meaning of "mysteries" when this word was employed in our text.

Essentially, we are having described to us that function of the Holy Spirit's work in our hearts, minds, and living, by which He brings our whole lives increasingly into the light—

- into the light of life in Christ,
- into the light of understanding God's Word,
- into the light of knowing ourselves, and
- into the light of more clearly perceiving others.

Most of us come to Christ with a thick residue of accumulation overlaying our hearts, minds, and attitudes. It's something like the geological strata of silt that is laid down by the flow of water over years and ages, forming the visible layers we see in the rocky formations in the mountains. But in our personalities, this silt is awaiting the rising and washing of a river from heaven to remove the residue of the past and to expose the wealth which, like gold in the mountains, is waiting to unfold with God's rich purposes for our lives. It is a distinct ministry of the Holy Spirit to do this, to flow into the inner recesses of our beings and to bring to the surface anything that would obstruct our growth in grace and remove it. He wants to help bring to the surface everything that would advance the Father's purpose in us but which has been buried by the turbulence or contrary streams of our past experiences or ignorance.

The silver-sided streamliner streaked eastward from Los Angeles, and Anna, the children, and I were enjoying the first hours of our long-planned train trip. Because fewer and fewer train experiences are being known by today's kids as jet travel has become so common and faster, we had made arrangements to take this vacation via the rails. The kids were loving it, not only taking in the scenes but especially enjoying the knowledgeable banter of the conductor who had paused midway in our car to talk with different ones of the passengers.

He had come to their aisle and leaned over, poking his aging finger toward the window.

"See the river there," he said, pointing to a broad dry river bed about a hundred yards away which paralleled our course.

The kids looked outside again, having seen nothing before, and then one of them ventured a challenge, supposing they were being teased. "There's no river there. At least not this time of year!"

The older man smiled back and said, "I know that's what it looks like, but let me tell you something, kids. That's the Mojave River—one of the most important rivers in the West. Y'all see how things are green all along the banks of what looks like a dry river bed to us?"

The children nodded, listening intently.

"Well, that's because there *is* a river there—and it's flowing right now—in fact, all year long. But most of the time it's about fifteen to twenty feet below the surface."

"Is there a tunnel or canal cut underneath there?" he was asked.

"No, it's just filtering through the sand and the rocks, but it is flowing—all the time. It's an unseen river right there in the desert, and it never stops."

Would you join me in connecting what we learned with our children that day to the analogy Jesus promises of rivers? Because here, in rivers like the one in the Mohave Desert, we can find yet another description of a Holy Spirit ministry available to us; a ministry which is advanced by the exercise of the spiritual language. This concept, applied to our text, suggests how the flow of the spiritual language may be applied in prayer to bring to the surface of our understanding things which have become hidden to our conscious mind. Let me illustrate.

I had been ministering for several days at a conference site in the picturesque Ozark Mountains. One morning following the worship service a camper asked if I would be willing to talk with him about a continuing heaviness and fear that shadowed his soul. I consented, and after lunchtime made my way to the office I'd arranged to use.

The first few minutes of our conversation were enough to make two things very clear: (1) he was sensible and sensitive to the Holy Spirit, and (2) indeed there was something which seemed to hinder his sense of peace and confidence as a believer. Because he was a mature Christian, the problem was not a lack of the Word of God. But there was something else. Some log jam of the soul was the picture the Holy Spirit was giving me. Seeing this prophetic picture, I said, "Have you ever seen pictures of a giant log jam on a river where loggers have been floating timber downstream? A tangle snarls the forward flow of the logs." He knew what I was depicting.

"Well," I explained, "that's the kind of picture I'm seeing right now, and I believe it's a picture of something in your past—something or some things that have happened which you don't consciously remember but which are tied like a knot in your soul."

He seemed to recognize that this is something that is common to most people, so I didn't need to assure him that he wasn't a strange or peculiar psychiatric case. I went on.

"You know, Jesus taught that the Holy Spirit's work in our lives would be like rivers—sometimes mighty surgings and at other times a quiet flowing—but always rivers of God's divine power moving within us." I then asked, "Do you have a regular exercise of the spiritual language?"

He confirmed that he did, so it was simple to move ahead.

"There is a beautiful promise about the spiritual language in 1 Corinthians 14—let me show it to you here—verse 2." I read it and explained how the Holy-Spirit-given language has a potential to solve mysteries; that is, "to bring into the light things that have been recessed in our subconscious." I told him how I had not only seen, but had experienced the ability of the Spirit of God to do in a matter of minutes what may take a trained psychologist or counselor dozens of private sessions or years of therapy. Then I gave this counsel.

"I'm going to pray briefly with you, right now. Then I'm going to step outside the office for ten minutes or so and leave you and the Holy Spirit alone." I smiled, "I like to call Him the Great Psychiatrist in moments like these. Just as we often call our Lord Jesus the Great Physician as He heals so marvelously and sometimes miraculously. The Holy Spirit has a very special healing ministry too. While I'm gone, I simply want you to be at prayer, for the most part, employing your spiritual language; allowing the presence of God to flow through your inner being." I added that I was recommending that he do this, not as a trick or a rote procedure I use (because I *never* approach *any* situation in a matter-of-fact way). But I urged this approach—was giving this counsel—because as we had prayed in fresh dependence upon the Lord for this conversation, this was the prompting the Counselor was giving.

He seemed comfortable with and understanding of what I had said, and so we joined hands and I prayed: "Father God, we come into Your presence through the Blood of Jesus Your Son, our Savior. This man is your son and my brother, and I thank You for the fact that all his sin has been covered at the Cross, and that the presence of the Holy Spirit within him is the seal of Your love and approval. Thank You for Your love for him—for us both, Lord." I paused and invited him to praise the Lord along with me for a few seconds, gratefully declaring thanks to God for His love and welcoming His power with worship.

"Now, Holy Spirit, I invite You to come into this room in a special way. Only You, Oh God, know the deep hindering or wounding things of my brother's past—things forgotten, but nonetheless present as obstacles to his fullest peace. I ask You that as he worships, praises, and prays, that You will bring to light any hidden, forgotten incidents which need to be dealt with. Do it with Your peace-giving presence, as I declare the dominion of Jesus' Name and the authority of His Kingdom. In Jesus' Name I also demand that no work of darkness have any part of this moment, and that all and any works of the flesh or the devil be removed by Your grace." I didn't really stop praying, I more or less withdrew, having told him that I would be leaving him after we began. I left as he continued praying, kneeling there beside the chair where he had been sitting.

There was nothing colorful or accomplished about what I did in the meantime. I suppose someone might think me insincere or not truly interested because of what I did next. For having stepped outside the office, onto the vast deck of the recreation area, and knowing the whole matter of this man's well-being was in the hands of the Great Psychiatrist, I ordered a Coke and played a game of ping-pong with one of the campers!

Several minutes later, I knocked at the door. He answered, inviting me in, and I opened the door to see a tear-washed face which had a look of genuine confidence. I could see by his countenance that something had happened.

"This is absolutely wonderful," he began. "I can hardly believe it, but in the last few minutes the Lord has brought back to my mind two events—one when I was about five years old and the other when I was about twelve. It seems incredible to me that I haven't consciously thought of them for years. In fact," he added, "I think I would have to say, I'd forgotten them."

He related the two episodes quite openly, describing two very traumatic kinds of things which would inevitably leave a scar on anyone's personality. But before he began to speak them, I said, "The speaking out of these events is important. So before you describe them, I want us to pray something which is even more important." I led in a prayer, something like this.

"Lord Jesus Christ, we stand in the light before Your Throne. You are our King and our God, and it is through Your Name and Your Blood that all authority has been given to You . . . and we are in awe that You have passed that authority over sin and darkness to us. Now, as my brother speaks each of the following words, descriptive of hurtful, sinful, and injurious things in the past, we agree that even as he speaks them—*while he is speaking!*—that these experiences will be completely loosed from his mind, his emotions, from his life! They are being brought into the light in Your presence and to You alone. And we ask that from this moment they shall be forever burned away by the glory of Your power, just as they have already been washed away by the cleansing of Your Blood. In Jesus' name, amen." ✓

He looked up from prayer. Expectancy abounding.

"Go ahead," I prompted, and he began to recite the incidents in the presence of Jesus Himself. He detailed in a tasteful way things that had been driven back into his subconscious for years. Because his youthful psyche had been so violated, his mind had chosen to bury the pain which it seemed unable to deal with, but now, all of it was being spoken to the Savior of all, whose merciful power was releasing each point where past pain had been nailed into his being.

When he was done, I prayed a prayer of closure on the past—binding those things *away* from ever again having a hold on his mind or being. Then, as we concluded, I added a precautionary word.

"You know," I began, "our common foe—the devil—may try once or twice to either tell you this won't make any difference, or to attempt to counterattack by trying to keep these incidents on your conscious mind—plaguing, accusing you with them. But you need to stand your ground, remembering and praisefully affirming where our Lord Jesus has put them: They have been put away . . . forever, under the Blood of the Cross! (Col. 2:14–15). If the devil tries either tactic, simply call on the Name of the Lord. Don't be afraid, and don't surrender even the slightest territory to the Liar. Remember, 'Who the Son sets free is free indeed!' Amen?"

"Amen!" he confirmed with a glow all over his countenance.

And it was a lasting glow which was ignited there that day, because I experienced a pleasant surprise following this encounter; a confirmation of this day's victory which was testified to about three or four years later.

I was addressing a convention in Kansas City—several thousand were present. And as I left the platform at the end of the meeting, a man waved and said, "Could I have one brief word with you, Pastor Hayford?" I thought I recognized the face, and though I wasn't sure, I told my companion, Steve, to wait a minute with me. (As always, one of the men on our pastoral staff was traveling with me.)

The man smiled. "I don't know if you remember me, but you prayed with me at . . . ," and even as he spoke, the scene came back to mind. I acknowledged as much, and he said: "I just wanted to say one thing. It's been more than three years, and everything is still great!" His smile, the glow still there, and the way he said "great!" were enough to convince and rejoice any Christian's soul. I expressed my praise to the Lord—gave him an affirming hug, and as Steve and I walked away my eyes misted with the thought of another testimony of how mightily God, by His Holy Spirit, has provided for the ongoing work of His Son to be advanced in our souls—whatever the need!

This isn't the only way the River of Unveiled Mysteries works. For further example, I can hardly number the times I have wrestled with a text of God's Word, seeking to gain insight into the Bible's holy truth in a way that will release its transforming power to the congregation I'll be addressing. Time and again, as I pray over Scriptures in my spiritual language—praying by the same Spirit who gave the Word initially—I've experienced the simplest-yet-most-wonderful thing. It's as though the light inherent in God's Word suddenly becomes freshly alive; as though a shaft of glory from His own lips has breathed into me the same way that same Breath first breathed the words on His sacred pages. The Word will almost explode into refreshing insight at times, and on other occasions gradually open like a doorway spilling splendor into an unlighted room.

I have also found dynamic attitudinal changes occur as I have prayed for people—for troubled or troubling individuals—praying in my spiritual language. And often, as I pray with both the spirit and the mind, the Spirit Himself will show mysteries—that is, bring to light things about the inner need of that particular person which changes my heart toward him or her and increases my patience and compassion.

My journey toward the heart of God has been marvelously advanced along the way by the means of this particular river. It's a resource everyone of us need and might well welcome for ministry, for insight, and for the ongoing correction and adjustment of our attitudes toward dear people whom we might see differently if the Holy Spirit flooded our minds with a brighter view—God's view of them.

Rivers of Power

> That God would grant you, according to the riches of His glory,
> to be strengthened with might through His Spirit in the inner man.
>   Ephesians 3:16

I had contemplated describing a fourth river but realized that in an unmistakable way the fact I wished to communicate relates to all the rivers of the Holy Spirit's workings. Paul's prayer in Ephesians 3 touches the heart of the matter. He prayed, literally, for each believer to become mighty by the Holy Spirit's power—"strengthened with might through His Spirit."

It is impossible to discuss the mightiness of the Holy Spirit without at some time coming to terms with the fact that He isn't tame. The truth of His dovelikeness has often been accentuated at the expense of His fire-and-wind likeness. He is gentle and tenderly sensitive, but He is also Almighty God as well. There are times that the surgings of His river workings in our soul will be unmistakably mighty. He won't smother us with His power, but He will surprise us in a holy way.

The North Platte River is one of the large tributaries to the wild Missouri, which the lyricist describes in the classic frontier song, "Shenandoah." I "met" the North Platte—and I use the word advisedly—in a very memorable way, the year Anna and I were married.

We had traveled to Nebraska together shortly after our wedding. There were many of her large, Midwestern family who wanted to get to know their sweet daughter/sister/niece/cousin's groom, and of course, I had the joy of getting to know them that summer, too. But I hadn't planned on meeting the North Platte River.

Anna was raised, literally, on the banks of this great river. Her folks' property backed on it, and so she was brought up swimming, fishing, playing, and generally enjoying its benefits. So for old times' sake, one day during our visit, she and I—along with a couple of her brothers—went out back of the house and hiked back to the stream to wade, play, and swim. At first we splashed near the banks, but after a bit I ventured out a little further. And it was then, while nothing life-threatening occurred, I shall never forget what began to surround me, something I had never experienced before.

Having been raised in California, I'd often been into the surf and knew the power of the Pacific's waves driving against the shore. But in this moment, "meeting the North Platte," I suddenly discovered an unhurried but quiet power. All at once I noticed it: I was moving downstream. I was doing nothing, but *I was being moved!* It wasn't rapid, but inexorably . . . irresistibly . . . mightily, I was being carried. The sensation was almost frightening, not because I feared I would drown or because some eddy or undertow was grabbing at me, but because I felt so completely at the mercy of the mightiness of the river. I could get out, but I couldn't control it!

This wasn't a swimming pool, nor was it the ocean. Instead, I found out something about rivers: Once you're committed to the river's current, you're going to go somewhere!

Think on that with me. Fearlessly.

Think on it in wonder—of God's loving mightiness.

For it is in the light of this "meeting" with the North Platte River that I am wanting to beckon you, dear reader, to an openness to whatever dimensions of the Holy Spirit's workings which He might like to introduce to your circle of acquaintance.

Who wouldn't want to be open to the River's flow!

Where rivers flow there is growth; the stream nurtures and enriches. Where rivers flow there is a steady change of scenery; life doesn't settle for the status quo, there's movement—forward movement. Where rivers flow there is beauty, there is refreshing, and there are both peace and power in their season.

I had gone alone to the sanctuary one Saturday night. Feeling drawn to a special time of prayer for the services to take place there the next day, I began—as my custom often is—to walk from seat to seat and pray. Anticipating the many who would be seated there and longing for a ministry of the Spirit distinct to each one's need, to everyone, I prayed earnestly, invoking a special flow of God's grace.

That evening, having completed my row-by-row coverage of more than two thousand seats, I had moved to the platform for prayer. As I paced back and forth, with a sudden rise of mightiness like the surges of the North Platte that day, I felt myself—from deep within—being summoned to mighty shoutings and loud songs of prayer and praise.

The room echoed to my voice. I didn't *have* to cooperate with the swelling that rose within me, but if I were going to pray the way the

Spirit was moving me, I needed to let go, to give place to the only way a human being could adequately express the strength, the passion, the force, and the might that was rising from within.

I began to sing loudly in the Spirit. And I clapped my hands and would intermittently shout my soul's cry for more of God and more of His working. Had anyone been present, I would probably have been reluctant to allow such outright shoutings as those to which I yielded in response to the inward surgings of God that I felt. Were a videotape available of those moments that evening, I doubt you would be embarrassed—nor would I. Anyone would simply recognize that this was not a fanatic departing on a tangent to the bizarre, but that there was pointed passion directed toward purposeful prayer. The next morning, the evening's awakening of my soul became interpretable.

There were scores of souls brought to Christ.

There was a mightiness in the message that stirred everyone beyond the usual workings of God's grace among us.

It was clear to see that God had a plan for the day that transcended the usual. And it was Him—the Holy Spirit in Person—who sovereignly stirred my soul with both a passion for prayer and an enablement in prayer. Yet as surely as I was being drawn to and enabled for prayer, as the spiritual language became a distinct part of that enablement, I had to decide: Will I allow the rivers to surge within, or try and tame God to suit my tastes?

It's the decision every sojourner pursuing the heart of God has to make.

The grandness of God's River of Life-in-the-Spirit, and the multiple rivers that course from their fountain, invites us all to its beauty, its blessing, and its mightiness.

But each of us will be the one to decide unto *what* and unto *how much* we will commit of this mightiness and beauty.

9

For the Promise Is to You

> "You shall receive the gift of the Holy Spirit. For the promise is to you and to your children, and to all who are afar off, as many as the Lord our God will call."
>
> Acts 2:38–39

*I*t's decades ago now, but the combination of nervous trepidation and heart-filled affection joined to pure youthful passion easily returns it all to memory. It was the night I asked Anna to marry me.

Even though we had only been seeing one another seriously for about two months, and although I knew a wedding would be out of the question for nearly two years, I also felt sure that this was the woman the Heavenly Father had arranged for me. Though we were young, we both had been privileged with a solidity poured into our backgrounds. Having been raised by Christian parents and trained to know and seek God and walk in response to His Word's commands and the Holy Spirit's call, we had been given footings with which many young couples are unblessed. Further, we both were called to public ministry.

Weeks of deep conversation had revealed a commonality of understanding about each of our lives' purpose and begotten in our hearts a warmth of blossoming love for one another. And even though our exchanges had sometimes hinted at the prospect of a possible future together, I felt—I *knew* there needed to come a time—a moment "when it is said," when a mutual commitment would be sealed.

The tenderness of the memory would not be despoiled were I to relate more completely how I asked, nor would she or I be unwilling to describe the details. But I have opened with just this much recollection because that situation was not unlike this moment in this book.

There is something I wish to ask more specifically of you, dear friend. And it is surprisingly very much parallel to Anna's and my relationship before the night I asked. You see, on any issue of potential consequence to our lives:

- Each of us can meet a truth as well as a person.
- We can grow in understanding and feel attracted.
- We can believe there's a future in relationship.
- We can know that we're on safe ground because of solid, biblical background.
- We can know it's time to act—"that it be said."

All in all, my writing finally brings me to the question: "Will you marry the truth we've examined? Are you prepared to commit to a life together?"

Welcoming Spiritual Language

Of course, the truth to which I refer is the one which I have testified to and which we have discussed together through these pages. Do you agree that it's been sensibly and practically integrated with the basics of mainstream Christian life? Because I've hoped to make clear that the spiritual language is not peripheral, not an isolated subject, but a vital part of the broad body of "the truth as it is in Jesus" (Eph. 4:21).

I think our priorities have been kept clear, too, don't you? As we've dealt with this precious and significant facet of the Christian life, we have:

- Emphasized the centrality of Jesus Christ and His Cross in all things and our call as disciples to walk purely and faithfully with Him.
- Affirmed the finality and sufficiency of the Scriptures to guide our lives, guard us from error, and give us our daily supply of heavenly manna for growth and nourishment.
- Demonstrated our commitment to the unity of the Body of Christ by dealing with this truth in the Holy Spirit of love for all the brothers and sisters of every Christian tradition.

In that climate, we've walked together along the pathway I was asked to trace—my journey toward the heart of God.

I've described how along that pathway I've discovered the beauty, bounty, and blessing of a biblical, God-given resource in the spiritual language—speaking with tongues. In sharing this pilgrimage, I think I've explained the most practical and powerful discovery I made; that is, the assistance of this prayer form in praise and worship, as well as prayer and intercession's warfare in the spiritual realm. But perhaps the most liberating thing I discovered was that this heaven-sent benefit is available to every believer who would welcome it.

In short, I believe God wants you, me—every Christian—to know that this blessed benefit comes without sectarian requirements or doctrinaire qualifications. The only requirement is that, within our faith in Christ, we express our hunger and thirst for more of God's grace, that we welcome the Holy Spirit to satisfy our quest and then openly receive this resource promised within His Kingdom joys. Such a quest is, in actuality, a quest for more of Jesus' own workings by His Spirit. And that's why I'm so happily bold to call you forward now.

You see, I still have one chapter to tell you of a recent trip—a story I want to narrate (with the message I was privileged to bring on that occasion). And I look forward to doing so because it's an opportunity to tell you even more about how wonderful I believe Jesus is. For *above* all, He is all there *really* is *after* all!

However, before doing that, it seems that right now is the time to invite you to welcome the spiritual language into your own experience. Perhaps you are already a continual participant in this beautiful blessing. Or maybe your testimony is, "I once spoke with tongues but didn't know ways or practical reasons for continuing." Or maybe fears, criticisms, or the antics of some person or group caused you to become disenchanted. But in any case, if a Holy-Spirit-enabled prayer language is not already a continuing part of your life presently, I want to issue this invitation in a manner just as uncluttered here as our focus has been all along the way.

In other words, I want you to receive something from Jesus Himself. This invitation is ultimately His, and the experiences He invites us to are really not given from the hand of another mere human. If I can encourage you to simply draw near to the Lord, I think you'll be free of any preoccupying concerns that could distract from an otherwise beautiful moment.

By that, I mean I want you neither (1) to feel you must speak with tongues to prove anything; nor (2) to feel you have failed if you ask the Lord Jesus and you don't speak with tongues immediately.

But I must be honest with you: I do pray that you will ask Him to overflow your soul with new dimensions of praise and prayer, and I do ask Him—prayerfully agreeing with you—that you will receive a release into the beauty of spiritual language.

Let me give you some suggestions for walking forward toward this meeting with our Lord Jesus—for it is to *Him* we come. He is the One who dispenses the Holy Spirit in full measure to our lives. While the Holy Spirit is the distributor of the gifts He gives, our Savior is the only one—the Ultimate One—who ministers all matters concerning our experiences with and in the Holy Spirit. In the same way John the Baptist said Jesus was the only Savior, "Behold, the Lamb of God, who takes away the sin of the world" (John 1:29); he also announced, "This is He who baptizes with the Holy Spirit!" (John 1:33).

"But Jack," you might ask, "are you saying I haven't been baptized in the Holy Spirit if I haven't yet received my spiritual language?"

My quick answer to you is, "No, I am not saying that."

The relationship between Holy-Spirit-fullness and the Holy-Spirit-enabled language is so close in its appearance in the Bible that some of us (like me, in the past) considered them synonymous because they are so often simultaneous. But as I told you in chapter 6, I now find myself incapable of saying you (or anyone else) has or hasn't been filled with the Holy Spirit—especially if you *know* that you've met the Savior in Holy Spirit baptizing or infilling fullness.

What I am doing now, however, is pointing the way to this overflowing fullness in that particular and privileged aspect afforded us, to a language that offers new dimensions of worship and praise. And in that quest it is Him—our dear Savior Jesus—whom you will want to encounter and embrace in such a moment.

Steps to Take

First, whenever I talk with anyone who is asking anything from God, I will usually help them be sure of a clear conscience before Him. John wrote, "Beloved, when our hearts condemn us not, we have confidence toward Him" (1 John 3:21); so confession of any known sin is the best way to start.

Clear your heart of any muddied question marks.

Bring any guilt, failure, neglect, or condemnation you feel under the Blood of Jesus.

In prayer apply and then declare 1 John 1:7, 9:

> But if we walk in the light as He is in the light, we have fellowship with one another, and the blood of Jesus Christ His Son cleanses us from all sin. . . . If we confess our sins, He is faithful and just to forgive us our sins and to cleanse us from all unrighteousness.

Second, it is always wise to precede requesting anything from the Lord with any needed prayers of forgiveness to others. Just as you have *been forgiven*, having asked God's forgiveness, be certain that you *are forgiving*. Be sure there are no hardened places in the soul where you are consciously withholding a generous spirit of forgivingness toward anyone, any human being who may have hurt, shown misunderstanding, or violated you in any way, at any time.

This could, in fact, be the most important thing that happens to you in taking these steps.

A mound of obstacles often surrounds many a devoted Christian who has accumulated an unwieldy burden of anger or pain toward another or others. Walls may have been built and yet never come to terms with. It could involve only one person. That one person may even be someone very dear to you, yet one whose words or actions have sorely pierced your soul—whether intentionally or unintentionally. Our fullest release in the worship of our Lord, and the joy of being liberated in a new language of prayer and praise, could even be hindered or blocked by unforgiveness. Or worse, unresolved residual bitterness will eventually find a way to embitter the flow of this new river of blessed resourcing in the Holy Spirit. Even were spiritual language to be released to you, there is no shortcut around these spiritual basics. So settle such matters with God. Now.

Speak to the Lord the names of anyone you need to forgive. Confess your pain or offense over what happened. Acknowledge any failure you recognize on your part, however difficult it may be to admit it. Then, lay it all—totally—at Jesus' feet. Do it *now*.

Begin with worship.

Let praise rise to God for the fact that He has forgiven you and me of greater things than anyone has ever done to us. Do this wholeheartedly, because it's true. However heinous the hurtful deeds of others may have been, our sins against God are vastly greater than human-to-human sins, because we have all also sinned against Him. Yet, still, praise His Name! Because He has totally forgiven us—and in that joyful confidence let us freely and totally forgive others! I'm sure that neither you nor I ever want to hear our Lord say to us,

> You wicked servant! I forgave you all that debt because you begged me. Should you not also have had compassion on your fellow servant, just as I had pity on you?
>
> Matthew 18:32–33

Rather, in the same sweetness of the Holy Spirit with which we want Christ to overflow us, let us hear the word of the Lord:

> Freely you have received, freely give. . . . For everyone to whom much is given, from him much will be required.
>
> Matthew 10:8; Luke 12:48

> And do not grieve the Holy Spirit of God, by whom you were sealed unto the day of redemption. Let all bitterness, wrath, anger, clamor, and evil speaking be put away from you, with all malice. And be kind to one another, tenderhearted, forgiving one another, just as God in Christ also forgave you.
>
> Ephesians 4:30–32

As you deal with this, it may be that—amidst the brokenness of your confession and your yielding to a spirit of forgiveness—you may find yourself on the brink of speaking with tongues. I've often found this to be true in ministering to others. For it is in such moments of full humility and openness that the Spirit of God sweeps in, filling the space in our souls that has been emptied of unworthy matters.

Third, come with expectation, settled in your belief that God's Word assures that this promise is for you!

When Peter said at Pentecost, "For the promise is unto you, and to your children and to all that are afar off—even as many as the Lord our God shall call" (Acts 2:39), he was speaking of you and me—right up to this present moment! The promise to which he referred was clearly inclusive of all that his hearers had seen, heard, and asked about—"What does this speaking with tongues mean?" (Acts 2:1–13). As Peter preaches his answer, receptive respondents hear his message on the Holy Spirit's coming and have their question answered. Peter declares how Jesus' death, resurrection, and ascension proved His Lordship. Then he explains that now, as Messiah, Jesus is ready to give the Holy Spirit to them if they repent and believe in Him (Acts 2:14–37). He says, essentially, "You'll receive the same thing as these you have seen and heard" (Acts 2:33). So his listeners then asked: "What shall we do?" (Acts 2:37).

That's a question I am presuming you've asked before now. I'm assuming you have already obeyed God in at least two respects: (1) that prior to this you have repented of your sin and put your faith in Jesus Christ as your Savior; and (2) that you have been obedient to be baptized in water according to His command (Acts 2:38; Mark 16:16).[2]

Now it's on the grounds of our having obeyed in these ways that you and I thereby have every reason to expect the same thing those first believers received—for "the promise is unto you!"

The whole of this book in your hands has dealt with that aspect of the promise, that expression of God's fullness which offers us all the privilege and beauty of the spiritual language as an expanded enablement for prayer and praise.

That part of the promise is unto you, too!

As surely as your salvation, as surely as the Holy Spirit has come to indwell you, so surely is the spiritual language available with His fullness. *"For in Christ all the promises of God are Yes! and Amen! to the glory of God through us!"* (2 Cor. 2:20). So expect what He's promised. As surely as God's Word makes the promise, so surely will He answer your request. Hear what Jesus said:

> If a son asks for bread from any father among you, will he give him a stone? Or if he asks for a fish, will he give him a serpent instead of a fish? Or if he asks for an egg, will he offer him a scorpion? If you then, being evil, know how to give good gifts to your children, how much more will your heavenly Father give the Holy Spirit to those who ask Him!
>
> Luke 11:11–13

There it is, dear one. Jesus Himself promises that you will not be turned away with unsatisfaction, not be deceived by a demon, nor will you be rendered the pain of stinging rejection. Jesus is saying that Father God is going to see that you receive all that is holy and glorifying to Him.

Fourth, start praising Him now. Even as you read my words, begin to praise the Lord. Get on your knees if you are able at this moment, and:

- Let your upraised head express your faith in God's love to-ward you,

- Let your upraised hands express your openness to all He has for you, and

- Let your upraised voice begin with hallelujahs of gratitude and expectation for the presence and promise of all His Holy Spirit's fullness and overflow in your life.

If that spirit of faith and praise is present now, stop reading and go ahead. I'll still be here when you finish.

Beginning to Speak in Tongues

Years ago I heard a very gentle, yet exuberant minister as he was trying to help people who were open to the spiritual language but who had not yet found a release in their expressing this in prayer. Harald Bredesen, a man whose training for ministry and roots had been in the Dutch Reformed Church, put it this way. "You know," he said, "when I sought to open to the Spirit, I found myself so earnestly desirous of doing everything right, I actually got in the way of the holy naturalness with which the spiritual language is to be received and enjoyed." He proceeded to explain in a quite tasteful and unembarrassing way, likening this to his wedding night. "Both of us were virgins," Harald declared, "and I found myself so preoccupied with what was new—hoping not to violate anything proper, or in any way be insensitive to my wife—that I almost completely missed enjoying what was being given me to enjoy!"

When Harald shared this, laughter filled the room. The sweet innocence of his manner, as well as the pure childlikeness in the occasion itself, profoundly made a point which marvelously illustrates a difficulty that many of us have with regard to beginning with the spiritual language. But over the years I've learned that beginning to speak with tongues occurs in many different ways among the Lord's people. God's infinitely creative ways, along with each of our individual uniqueness in His plans, assures that such variety in experience will occur. For example:

- I described my sister's remarkable experience of speaking in a recognizable tongue, though not one she had learned.

- At the same campsite, though many years later, I saw a young woman lift her hands and begin worshiping in sign language. An observer who knew such signing began whispering the interpretation of what was being expressed—a beautiful stream of prose which was magnifying Almighty God.

- I once prayed with a man who had been a comedian, who in fact had become slightly cynical about the matter of Holy Spirit fullness. But when he began, speaking with tongues in a very limited way at first, in a few moments his whole being rocked with a soul-liberating laughter, an overflow that was in no way irreverent or silly. Rather, it was clear that all cynicism was being rinsed from him as a holy joyousness burst over his soul.

- I prayed with another man who remained completely silent after prayer, even though I encouraged his praise. He explained how his high church background made him still hesitant. Yet he also still avowed he was opened and as I had prayed with him, "Something . . . Someone" had touched his soul. A few days later he was on a trip, and while soaking in a bathtub in Beirut, Lebanon, a spirit of worship and thanksgiving rose, and he began to speak with tongues.

- Another man in our congregation came forward at a time of prayer for those who were opening to this dimension of fullness. As he later put it, "Nothing happened, but I did believe." Two days later he was sitting in his car, waiting for his children to get out of school, when a car accident took place before his eyes at the intersection. Immediately, he began to pray with concern for the situation, and as he did the language of the Holy Spirit began to rise with his intercession.

Accounts of various ways people have begun in their spiritual language could go on indefinitely, but the evidence is basically that there is no pattern of required response. The principal essentials are (1) our openness and faith, and (2) our being willing to speak. The spiritual language is not a seizure, but neither does it usually occur without some initiative on our part. Remember, "They . . . began to speak with

other tongues, as the Spirit gave them utterance" (Acts 2:4). The Holy
Spirit provides the linguistic ability, but you and I are the speakers. At
some point, faith needs to begin speaking.

I have frequently pointed out that spiritual language often occurs in a person's mind even before it is spoken. This is not uniformly
the case, but it is with sufficient frequency that two things should be
noted.

- First, this prompting should not be feared or doubted, but
  neither should it be sought or taught. We forbid people
  telling others, "Here, say these words to begin." This is not
  only tasteless and unscriptural, but it also violates the opportunity for the individual taking the faith step that he or
  she ought to take for themselves.

- Second, remember that your language may at first be quite
  simple. The beginning may not be dramatic or expansive,
  but if you begin in faith, then continue in faith. Trust the
  Lord to expand the language and be at peace in this: He
  will!

Another thing I have learned that has proven helpful to thousands
of Christians whom I have led toward a release into the beauty of spiritual language, is to sing your praises. By that, I simply mean to urge
that you sing your own song. The Psalmist says, "Sing unto the Lord a
new song," so let the melody be freely formed from your heart's worship. Even if you're a monotone, or if your voice is like gravel from
sickness, age, or abuse, it's still *your* voice—and God loves to hear *you!*
He isn't conducting a talent contest, He's welcoming opened, earnest
souls. So sing! The Bible says,

> Be filled with the Spirit, speaking . . . psalms and hymns and
> spiritual songs, singing and making melody in your heart to the
> Lord.
>
> Ephesians 5:18–19
>
> I will sing with the spirit, and I will also sing with the understanding.
>
> 1 Corinthians 14:15

Spiritual songs probably refer to songs whose lyrics are of Holy
Spirit origin, and the Scriptures evidence that God not only accepts
singing with tongues, He directs it in His Word.[2] Often, a human

reluctance to launch out into the spiritual language is overcome while praise is being wafted on the melody of a song.

By launching out I do not mean making up a language. I have never seen anyone foolish enough either to want or to attempt to do that. To the contrary, the exact opposite characterizes the sincere seeker who often is so fearful of doing something in the flesh that he or she is hesitant to even speak out with childlike beginnings.

But do. In a childlike way, be unafraid to begin to reach out for the language miracle that is awaiting you, remembering that the spiritual language *is* a miracle.

That's right. It's a transcending of the natural by the intervention of the supernatural grace of God. But that doesn't mean that you and I do nothing. Miracles usually await a human action to invite their manifestation.

- Moses held out a rod, and the sea opened (Exod. 14:16, 21).
- The priests stepped into the Jordan, and the water stopped (Josh. 3:13).
- Joshua spoke aloud for Israel to hear, calling for the sun to stand still, and God did the rest (Josh. 10:12–13).
- Peter answered Jesus' call and stepped out of the boat, and then the miracle of his walking on the water began (Matt. 14:25–29).

So, in the same faith-taking-action way, as you open to the miracle of the spiritual language, take the step God's Word directs. Speak. And according to the Scriptures, you may "speak with other tongues as the Spirit enables you with new languages."

Now, dear friend, I hope that by the time you have come to these words that you have not only come to believe the beauty of spiritual language is for you, but that you have received a beginning in this blessed resource given to us both. And further that your joy will be to welcome this ongoingly, realizing edification and an enhancement of your walk with Jesus as you continue with this tongue and all this unto a walk in deeper humility. That's the key to employing the increasing sense of authority in His Name you will discover. Humility before His throne and gratitude for His many graces will keep our perspective clear on the blessing of our spiritual language.

Continually pray.

Praise.

Worship.

And continually give forth the life and love of the Kingdom of God in all you do . . . wherever you go.

The ultimate test of the value of this holy, expanded utterance in our experience will be in our expanded obedience to, deepened devotion toward, and heightened gratitude for our Lord Jesus Christ. He is the center and the circumference of all our life, salvation, and service. And that's why any beautiful thing we receive in Him is that we may more beautifully serve Him, and all the more wonderfully adore the beauty of Him Himself.

Which leads me to conclude with telling you of my trip to Brighton.

10

The Ultimate Beauty—
The Uniqueness of Christ

One world lost in lovelessness;
One Name given in graciousness;
One Spirit reaching to join the two.

*T*hough it was July, it was a bleak, chilly afternoon as I wheeled my car onto Kingsway Boulevard near the east end of that portion of England's south coast where Brighton lies. I had just flown into Gatwick, south of London, about an hour before, and was now navigating toward the hotel where my accommodations had been arranged by the host committee for the International Charismatic Consultation on World Evangelism. More than twenty-seven hundred select delegates were gathering from scores of nations, representing virtually every Christian denomination on every continent. These were the leaders I was to address the next evening on the theme of "The Uniqueness of Christ," speaking to the challenge of keeping a faithful testimony of Jesus in an increasingly hostile environment.

Current observers of the world's religious scene have noted the growing insistence by non- or anti-Christian leaders and governments that believers in Jesus Christ temper their zeal for evangelism. Demands that we tone down our message, along with accusations of proselytizing, are rising everywhere. In a shrinking world, clashing religious beliefs are judged an unnecessary, undesirable addition to human tensions, and Christians have been the first to face the railing demands for silence. My assigned role in this conference was to address this challenge: How does a Holy-Spirit-filled believer stand firm in such a world? And further, amid sporadic accusations of doctrinal slackness which some Christians have attributed to charismatics, a clear declaration of our Christ-centered theology and practice was called for.

As I drove westward along the ocean front, the essence of the crucial nature of my message seemed suddenly to be illustrated before me. A haunting specter captured my gaze. Tottering above the windblown surf, like a shimmering mirage blending into the grayness of the low slung clouds scudding above the Atlantic's uninviting main, stood the remains of Brighton's South Pier.

In stark contrast to her counterpart a full mile to the east, where a bustling boardwalk bounced by day and glistened by night, South Pier lay dead. Here, stranded a hundred yards beyond the shoreline, elevated by hundreds of pylons supporting her massive perch fifty feet above the churning waves, this remnant of pretended magnificence seemed to weep over past glories.

How like humanity! I thought. Gutted by fire, the pier seemed to sulk, as though remembering the days when her decks echoed with dance music and swarmed with pleasure seekers. But now, emptiness stared from her broken windows like a thousand hollow eyes shadowed by soot. The remaining shell of the once splendid building seemed to attempt to straighten itself; a drunken derelict struggling to stand erect and square its shoulders to impress a passerby of a former dignity: "Doin' well, mate!"

My perception focused as though making a character study of the visible lamentation before me. I had parked my car now, but I couldn't pull myself from this scene. Somehow it evoked an emotion within me, a subtle sadness, an unuttered groan which had actually caused the slightest tremor of my chin: "South Pier (I had unconsciously referred to it as 'her') is a photograph of man's hopelessness."

A banner batted in the breeze across the gaping mouth of the massive section that had been torn open when the connecting structure between shore and pier had dissolved in flames. It had apparently been raised there by a team of hardy souls whose mission in life pursues the preservation of historic sites and endangered species. The giant graffiti-like lettering read, "Help! Save Me!" But the amassed demolition equipment on hand testified to the futility of the appeal. I thought it a summary statement of mankind's relentless efforts to build our dream sites—our careers, our relationships, our institutions, our reputations. How persistently we ply the piers of performance and pleasure, never really capturing more than a moment's titillating thrill ride of accomplishment or a mouthful of cotton candy's elusive sweetness. Then a crisis comes. How easily we succumb to burnout. How often we're left at sea, stranded, with charred bridges disallowing retreat. And how discontent constantly pounds like the waves at the footings of our soul, while sea gulls of circumstance croak their dirge of despair. Yet even then, how few will cry help, and how many, like the drunk, feign that all's well.

Everything within that scene depicted our world today. As I mused over South Pier's symbolism, my heart leaped within me at the prospective joy of bringing my message here. I reflected on the certainty that in heaven there is an Ear that hears and there is a Hand that reaches to rescue when hopeless hearts cry, "Save me!" God has no demolition crews. Only hell is apt at this art. And because of a Cross that was raised at an ancient site of skulls, there is a salvaging program for those derelict souls who will simply cry out, "Help!"

Later in my room, I reviewed my message, sure of its timeliness, thinking of a sagging pier across the street and its picture of our times. On one hand, God is pouring out His Spirit in unprecedented ways as hundreds of millions of Christians are opening to newness of life and the fullness of the Holy Spirit's power and love, readied by grace to reach the world with that message of God's mightiness. On the other, the world wallows on the waves of what may be history's final shoreline of despair, contriving its dreams of future repairs but still doomed by its rotting structures of God-resisting, pride-preserving sin and unbelief. Filled with these thoughts of mixed pathos and hope, I lay on my bed thinking on the conference and my message as I stretched my body from the kinks accumulated in fourteen hours of travel.

Distinctive to the conference was its charismatic context. Two common denominators linked the nearly three thousand conferees: (1) their commitment to the present ministry of the Holy Spirit's power, and (2) their passion to touch a hurting, dying world with God's love. Here was a band of people who knew the beauty of spiritual language and other attendant graces of the Holy Spirit. My mission was to help us unite our focus on how that blessing can expand vision and animate prayer to minister to our world the beauty of Jesus Christ in the power of Spirit-fullness. I sensed the essential need for a dual thrust: to point the way to a witness that would be both enabled and focused—enabled by our openness to the Holy Spirit, and focused on our call to minister powerfully in Jesus' wonderful Name. I felt a humanly helpless, humbly moving sense of honor to be allowed to bring such a message to so many outstanding leaders. Every heart here was bent toward glorifying Christ. All were joint seekers in finding how to do so with evangelistic effectiveness today.

The hours slipped by, and with a night's rest, my jet lag was left on the mattress. My assignment hour was now due. The early portions of the service saw the great congregation at worship. Next, a summary of the task in evangelizing people of Hindu and Muslim traditions was complemented by a thrilling report on the impact of the *JESUS* film in these and other settings. And then I was being introduced. As I stood, I heard my voice fill the congress hall as I brought personal greetings to the delegates. This is what I said.

The Conference Message[1]

I begin by confessing how humbling and how gratifying it is to be invited to minister God's Word to you, and especially on so marvelous a theme: The Uniqueness of Christ!

Surely those words state our highest priority. For first and foremost, as a band of pentecostal/charismatic leaders, if we've learned anything, we've found the Fountainhead of God's life, God's grace, and God's power—and it's in God's Son, Jesus our Lord!

Yes, it is true, that we are people who seek and welcome experiences in the Holy Spirit. But let everyone watching us know that above all blessing and beyond all experiences, most of all and first of all, we are people who want to praise Jesus, to glorify Jesus, to magnify Jesus, to exalt Him as our Living Lord and King! Christ is what we're about and all we're about!

Contrary to what some may think, the taste of new wine has not simply made us drunk with power. Rather, the Holy Spirit has ignited the fires upon our heart's altar with a warm, childlike first love for Jesus.

He's the reason for any fruitfulness we've found, for Jesus is the Vine.

He's the reason for the rivers of blessing from which we drink, for Jesus is the Fountain of Living Water.

He's the reason for our rejoicing, for having found Jesus precious, we praise Him with joy unspeakable and full of glory!

We are His—we're Jesus' own people. We have tasted the answer to St. Richard's prayer, as Jesus Himself has become clearer, dearer, and nearer to us!

Christ Himself is what we've found!
Let everyone hear it. Our treasure and testimony is:
    not gifts of power;
    not signs and wonders;
    not miracles of healing;
    not tongues, interpretations and prophecies;
    not church growth and mass evangelism success.

Oh, we've experienced those things—yes! But what we have found more than ever and more than anything is Jesus! Jesus Himself!

And I begin by underscoring this central focus of the charismatic movement, because if there is anything unique about what God is doing among us, it is all and only due to the uniqueness of the One we exalt among us—our Lord Jesus Christ. And His uniqueness is my assigned topic.

We all welcome fresh opportunities to extol His Majesty! Still, as joyous as it feels to be asked to lead this conference in focusing on Him, I am somewhat hesitant. I'm hesitant because each one of you—everyone of you—know Him so well, how could anyone add anything? Better that I would simply stand aside and say, "Let's just all kneel down together. Let's just look to Jesus." For in five minutes alone with Him by ourselves, we can gain more than in hearing hours of exposition about Him.

But it is doubtless unquestionably wise that our conference has chosen to make a corporate focus on Christ in this way, providing opportunity for a collective declaration on the biblical revelation of Christ's uniqueness.

I see at least three reasons to do so, reasons which relate to: (1) an ever-broadening circle; (2) an ever-watching sector; and (3) an ever-present disposition present today. In focusing on the Person of Christ, let me first focus on the ever-broadening circle of fellowship which the streams of today's acts of the Holy Spirit are drawing together in Jesus' Name.

An Ever-Broadening Circle

We are here from around the world and from throughout the whole Body of Christ. Our backgrounds are broad and diverse, and we are laced through with widely divergent doctrinal, liturgical, and methodological differences. But even though we hold widely varied opinions on church government, baptism, the Lord's Table, or differences on prophecy, last things, and Millennial interpretations, there is one overarching theme to which we rally in complete unity, and that's to the magnificence of Jesus Christ our Lord. We chorus uniform praise to the excellence of His Nature and the perfection of His Work.

Throughout history, these have been the watershed points for the church's life: who Christ is and what He's done. And as the church has stood upon Christ, so the church has grown in Him and with His blessing and presence.

- Only as Jesus Christ is central in the heart and mind of the believer, as God's only Son and our only Savior,

- Only as His Person and Authority dominate our life and our service—

Then and only then are we safe from confusion of purpose. So it is there and only there—around Jesus Christ—that any unity becomes a real, heaven-sent blessing, rather than a mere humanistic camaraderie.

I begin with this point: that the uniqueness of Jesus is the reason for the unity so abundantly present in the pentecostal/charismatic revival, because this phenomenon—our unity—puzzles some other Christians.

Some think our love for one another to be a spineless lack of convictions borne of theological or intellectual sloppiness. They seem to think our speaking with tongues has scrambled our brains and rendered us helpless to remember our doctrinal distinctives. Some treat us as though we were indifferent to any truths other than those of charismatic specialty, and that that narrowness explained our community. But may I affirm, once and for all, our unity is *not* the result of theological passivity. Our unity is neither a sacrifice of personal views nor a casual syncretism of homogenized and sifted doctrines producing a lowest-common-denominator theological swill.

Never!

Instead, our unity is a testimony to the uniqueness of the Holy Spirit's work in glorifying Jesus. You see, when the Comforter comes, He has a way of making you comfort-able with all people in whom He dwells. When the One whose mission is to glorify Jesus overflows you, you suddenly find yourself becoming an answer to His prayer, "That they may be one." And in the wake of becoming an answer to Christ's intercession, yet another prayer begins to blossom into life:

> For this reason I bow my knees to the Father of our Lord Jesus Christ, from whom the whole family in heaven and earth is named.
> Ephesians 3:14–15

Hear it! The apostle Paul's whole prayer is for Spirit-filled unity, and it has a way of happening in us when we put Jesus Himself in the center of our focus. Just as Paul's full heart cry to God hopes it may be, Ephesians 3:17–19 transpires inside each of us.

1. The fragrance of Christ's uniqueness is manifested as His Spirit dwells in our hearts (Eph. 3:17).

2. Becoming rooted and grounded in love, we begin to be "able to comprehend with all the saints what is the width and length and depth and height" (Eph. 3:18).

3. We begin "to know the love of Christ which passes knowledge" as we find ourselves being "filled with all the fullness of God" (Eph. 3:19).

This Christ-begotten lifestyle surges forward—from Ephesians 3 into Ephesians 4, from theory and prayer into life, love, and practice. As the apostle also urged, you find yourself "endeavoring to keep the unity of the Spirit in the bond of peace"—and for a grand and biblical reason. Hear it, please: "The unity of the Spirit" (Eph. 4:3) is what produces our "unity of the faith" (Eph. 4:13a). And it's centered on the only solid foundation for true unity: "the knowledge of the Son of God" (Eph. 4:13b).

There is the center which attracts our unity—knowing Jesus! He is the foundation for our unity.

We have found our individual entities, polities, and theologies to be infinitely inferior to the uniqueness of Christ Himself. In magnifying Christ's grandeur and glory as the Holy Spirit overflows our hearts, a truly biblical unity of the faith is discovered, not as a resolution of all doctrinal differences but as a revelation of the Living Word Himself— Jesus our Lord. He overflows our minds as well as our hearts, and in that flow we learn more than ever how to "speak the truth in love." The Holy Spirit has a way of glorifying Jesus in our hearts, a way which warms, which unifies our attitudes toward all others who know Him. Knowing Jesus as He really is and for all He really is begets an ever-expanding circle of fellowship among Christians today.

This must be what 2 Corinthians 5:16 means: "Therefore, from now on, we regard no one according to the flesh." Paul seems to be saying, "Having come to know Jesus, we have chosen to know one another only in Him—in Christ—and to sustain our fellowship around the glory of His Person." It's around the uniqueness of Christ that our unity is begotten and nourished by the Holy Spirit: His glory humbles us, His grace molds us, and as the Holy Spirit magnifies Jesus among us—beyond our private brands of Christianity—He draws us into a will to be "one."

Only Jesus could do this!

The uniqueness of Christ is the explanation for—indeed, the grounds of—this ever-broadening circle of fellowship being discovered among charismatics as well as others who are allowing the Holy Spirit to warm their hearts today unto new dimensions of fellowship.

An Ever-Watching Sector

But beside and beyond this ever-expanding circle of unity there is an ever-watching sector. It is constituted of that sizable body within Christian tradition who are waiting, watching, and still wondering where the charismatic movement may go.

Multitudes in every part of the church are standing at the river's edge of Holy Spirit renewal, curious and thirsty, wanting to test the waters. But many are often understandably hesitant even to dip a toe, much less plunge to a full spiritual immersion. First, they seek, want, and deserve an assurance that the tides of a spiritual renewal will not wash away their moorings of sound doctrine. So, for these as well, we lift this testimony. In focusing on Jesus Himself, we are making a declarative definition of what we see as foundational to all truth. In focusing on Him, we evidence that foremost to everything we love and live for, and undergirding all to which we testify and experience, is the Christ of the Bible.

What do we believe about Jesus?

I think I'm safe to speak for us all, for what I declare we not only hold in common. It's what the church has always said wherever a trustworthy, full-orbed testimony has been borne since the church's beginning.

When we say: Jesus Christ is Unique, we mean:

- He is the One and Only—the Second Adam sent to salvage and restore what the First Adam lost.
- He is the Virgin-born Son of God, sinless Man, the Incarnate Truth, the manifest fullness of the Father.
- He is the substitutionary Lamb of God—broken, bleeding, and dying according to the Scriptures; given to redeem from sin all who believe.
- He is the Crucified One who was buried and who rose again on the third day—literally, physically, and in power, according to the Scriptures.

And we say,

- Jesus is the One and only One who, providing the grounds of all human redemption, has now ascended to heaven, and who alone has then taken His seat at the right hand of the Father—all power in heaven and earth now having been given to Him upon the throne!

And we say, He is uniquely the One . . .

- The One who from upon that throne has poured out the Holy Spirit to all those who obey Him.
- The One who at that throne is ever living to make intercession for us.
- The One who from that throne will come again as King of kings and Lord of lords, to receive His redeemed church to be with Him forever.

Those are one-and-only things about Jesus! He is unique. There's no one else like Him!

- Soldiers sent to capture Him returned saying: "We've never heard any man speak like this man."
- Disciples witnessing His stilling the storm said: "What manner of man is this, that even the wind and the sea obey Him?"

- The Roman centurion watching Jesus die declared: "Surely this man was the Son of God."

The testimony to Christ's uniqueness abounds. Like Thomas, bowing before Him with every doubt settled, we say of the resurrected King, "You are my Lord and my God!" Don't you want to praise Him again and again? Go ahead! Let us stop here and do that . . . Amen! Hallelujah!

Let Us Further Elaborate Christ's Uniqueness

We live, as the church always has, in times when some would barter with truth to gain social acceptance. But in our elaboration of the Person of our Lord, let there be no confusion: Here are five crucial specifics to which we hold as unique to Jesus Christ.

1. He Is Unique as Creation's Source. We declare that Jesus Christ is unique among all human beings ever born on this planet. Though He entered creation, we hold that He preceded and exceeds it; that He is the Creator of all things. He is the *logos*—the Word; Second Person of the Godhead. We affirm John's testimony of Him:

> In the beginning was the Word, and the Word was with God, and the Word was God. He was in the beginning with God. All things were made through Him, and without Him nothing was made that was made.
>
> John 1:1–3

Further, we worship Jesus Christ not only as Creation's Source, but as its Sustainer. We believe that everything which exists is literally held together and upheld by the same word of power that He spoke in creating all things; that all that is and continues to be owes its existence to and is a tribute to Jesus' unique role as Creation's Source (Col. 1:16–17; Heb. 1:3).

2. Jesus Is Unique as God's Son. We declare that Jesus Christ is the only revelation of God to mankind in human form; that,

> The Word became flesh and dwelt among us, and we beheld His glory, the glory as of the only begotten of the Father, full of grace and truth.
>
> John 1:14

We assert, while "no one has seen God at any time," that Jesus, as the only begotten Son, has come from the bosom of the Father and "He has declared Him" (John 1:18). We contend that to see Jesus is to see all the fullness of the Godhead, bodily revealed; that as He said to Philip, so we testify: "He who has seen Me has seen the Father." Jesus is uniquely the Son of God as the revealer of the Father to mankind (John 14:9).

3. We Declare That Jesus Is Unique as Mankind's Savior.

> His alone is the blood that can redeem!
> His alone is the sacrifice that can satisfy the price of
>   sin's atonement!
> His alone is the body broken for our healing!
> His alone is the death that can purchase life for sinful
>   man!
> His alone is the righteousness that can justify us before
>   God and secure our not guilty verdict in His
>   court!
> His alone is the power that can break the chains of
>   death—for it was not possible that He could be
>   held by it! And,
> He alone, in rising, has verified to us the promise of
>   eternal life!

We trumpet His uniqueness here above all: Jesus alone can save! Neither is there salvation in any other, for there is no other Name under heaven given among men by which we must be saved! (Acts 4:12).

4. Jesus Alone Is the Church's Head and Its Chief Shepherd. Jesus alone is Head of the church. Having bought it with His blood, He alone has the right to rule it.

- He alone is the church's Foundation, "for no other foundation can anyone lay than that which is laid, which is Jesus Christ" (1 Cor. 3:11).

- He alone is the church's Builder, for He has said, "*I* will build My church and hell's counsels shall never prevail against it" (Matt. 16:18, emphasis added).

- He alone is the church's Life, for "as the branch cannot bear fruit of itself, unless it abides in the vine, neither can you, unless you abide in Me" (John 15:4).

Jesus Christ is the Founder of the church. But he is more to her—He is also Jehovah-Raah, the Redeeming Lord who *shepherds* His redeemed flock. Just as He is the slain Lamb who saves us, He is the Great Shepherd who keeps and governs us.

He is the church's Lord. For its proper exercise, we say that all authority in the church is solely derived from His headship, can only be received under His lordship, and must always be in the servant-spirit of His rulership: "He who would be greatest among you, let him be the servant of all" (Matt. 23:11). These are our Chief Shepherd's words, and as the sheep of His pasture we declare our absolute obedience to Him who uniquely is the leader and feeder of the church—His flock.

5. Jesus Christ Is Unique as Heaven's Appointed Sovereign. Sovereignty is common in our world. Not only do states, nations, kingdoms, and governments exercise sovereignty's absolute self-rule, but so does every single individual among all humankind. The right to self-government—to complete self-determination—is a God-endowed privilege invested in each human being.

Sovereignty abounds.

Indeed, it's humankind's misuse of sovereignty that is at the core of the human dilemma. And this makes it all the more important that we identify the uniqueness of Christ's Sovereignty.

Jesus Christ is uniquely Heaven's appointed Sovereign, for as creation's Source, as God's only Son, as mankind's Savior, as the church's Builder and Shepherd, Jesus is also the King of the universe and the ultimate Judge of every being in the entire cosmos.

- It is before Him all mankind will appear for review and judgment (Acts 17:31).

- It is by Him every believer will be approved or disapproved (2 Cor. 5:10).

- It is unto Him that every being shall ultimately bow the knee, and that every tongue shall consummately confess that Jesus Christ is Lord to the glory of God the Father (Phil. 2:9–11).

Let every ear hear it! This is what we believe about Jesus, and this is how we confess His uniqueness: We say of Him and we say to Him,

You are the Christ, the Son of the Living God. You alone are Source, Son, Savior, Shepherd, and Sovereign.

And if you wish, add to that, "Hallelujah, Jesus! Best of all, I am Yours and You are mine!"

Thus, as an ever-broadening circle of fellowship, however diverse our distinctives and differences, we affirm our common bond under the Unique Person of Jesus Himself. And to an ever-widening sector within Christian tradition which may be seeking assurance as to the charismatic renewal's convictions about Christ Himself, we offer this summary statement:

- We affirm the inexorable declarations of God's Word regarding His Son, His Person, and His Work. Here is unshakable terrain for any who seek a freer, fuller walk in the power of the Holy Spirit.

- We announce our interminable aspirations to exalt Him. Small wonder that praise and worship so characterize charismatics! When Jesus is clearly seen and fully surrendered to, the Holy Spirit will always ignite new dimensions of adoration and exaltation. As at Pentecost, our tongues extol the wonderful works of God. And there's no greater wonder than His having sent us Jesus!

An Ever-Present Disposition

But with these affirmations, we must address one conclusive aspect of Christ's uniqueness, and I do so with a very measured concern. Along with the glory of His Person, there are the inescapable implications in the uniqueness of Jesus Christ.

We live in a day with an ever-present disposition for delusion. Everywhere Jesus' own prophecy is being fulfilled: "Then many false prophets will rise up and deceive many. . . . Many shall come saying here is Christ or there is Christ; and because lawlessness will abound, the love of many will grow cold" (see Matt. 24:11–12, 23).

In this environment you and I have a demanding task. We are commissioned to preach His uniqueness in an era which has cynically been dubbed post-Christian. We are appointed to declare the gospel of His salvation in a society in which our holding to His uniqueness is deemed as arrogance.

It's a delicate point for us in dealing with our mission to evangelize the world.

How can we at once be perceived as coming in the spirit of Jesus—with compassion, forgiveness, understanding, and grace—while holding firm to the testimony of Jesus, that He alone is the Savior, and that outside Him there is no eternal salvation? Has God afforded a unique means for declaring Christ's unique Person to a world uniquely resistant to any such absolutes?

I think so.

I think a key for our times lies in a renewed discovery of the Holy Spirit's essential ministry as the spirit of prophecy. Let me explain.

Among the many aspects of New Testament life that have characterized the charismatic renewal is a new appreciation for prophetic ministry. By "prophetic ministry" I'm not speaking of sensational interpretations of last things. I'm referring to the testimony of Jesus which God's Word says is "the spirit of prophecy" (Rev. 19:10). I'm saying that the Holy Spirit outpouring in our times is suited to equip the church for our times. Just at the point where the church's institutional presence is being more deeply resented and resisted by political and religious systems, the Holy Spirit is moving to empower a new individual presence. The Spirit of prophecy is freshly qualifying multitudes for prophetic ministry; that is, ministry in the biblical sense of prophecy—proclaiming, unveiling, and renewing.

- First, prophecy is proclaiming. Just as at Pentecost the promise to the Spirit-filled was, "All my sons and daughters shall prophesy"; so today the Holy Spirit is seeking to renew every believer as a spokesperson for the gospel of the Kingdom (Acts 1:5–8).

- Second, prophecy is unveiling. Just as 1 Corinthians 14:24–25 shows how prophecy can penetrate the secrets of human hearts and bring unbelievers to their knees, so today the Holy Spirit is seeking to renew every believer as a potential discerner of people's pain, need, and burden.

- Third, prophecy is renewing. 1 Corinthians 14:1–5 says that all prophecy encourages, exhorts, and edifies; that it has an upbuilding way about it. So today, the Holy Spirit is seeking to renew every believer as an instrument of encouragement, uplifting the fallen in a failing world.

I propose that the church—not as an institutional presence, academically, politically, or ecclesiastically, but as a multitude of millions of Holy-Spirit-filled prophesiers—is being retooled for last-days ministry. Much like the first century, when a Holy-Spirit-empowered host overcame, though disallowed social access or political enfranchisement, we are simply being recalled to bear testimony to Jesus, renewed to simply, one-to-one, to lift Him up to hurting people by speaking the truths of His uniqueness into their personal circumstance. The world's structures may resist ours, but the world's spirit can't resist God's! Society may oppose and restrict the church's formal presence, but it can't control its personal presence.

In today's resistant environment, I propose that our best resource for evangelism is not by arguing with an unbelieving world, but by a fresh anointing of the Holy Spirit of prophecy. I submit that our primary challenge is to avoid entrapment in arguing philosophies, debating cults, or seeking political recognition. Since the Holy Spirit has come in power, we have all the enablement necessary to penetrate the world at the point God has assigned us to do so—at the personal level to every individual in every land.

We also have a model for doing this. It's Jesus Himself. And the Holy Spirit empowering us will also show us how to register the testimony of Jesus in the same winsome spirit of prophecy which He did.

Look at how Jesus evangelizes. His firm words of truth are unshakeable, but His gracious words spoken in love are completely disarming. He walks a line of unbelievable balance:

- He disavows judgmentalism as His mission, saying to His critics: "You judge according to the flesh; I judge no one. And yet if I do judge, My judgment is true" (John 8:15–16).

- He avows faithfulness to divine justice as His task, yet He says to a broken soul, "Neither do I condemn you; go and sin no more" (John 8:11).

- He expresses the fact and the price of both eternal gain and eternal loss; yet preachiness is absent in His way as He says, "God so loved the world that He gave His only begotten Son, that whoever believes in Him should not perish but have everlasting life" (John 3:16).

Here is the spirit of Jesus presenting the testimony of Jesus. That union of truth with tenderness is the blend I think He has called us to make in presenting His uniqueness to a blinded world.

I am persuaded that the same outpouring of the Holy Spirit which has begotten renewal and revival has also introduced a refreshing possibility for fulfilling our present mission to evangelize. The way we can address our world both confrontively and compassionately, and do it like Jesus, is by the spirit of prophecy! We are not commissioned to argue with people but to proclaim a Person. As we bear the testimony of Jesus, the Holy Spirit of prophecy will penetrate hearts, unveil their need, convince them of the adequacy of the Lord Jesus Christ, and draw people to Him.

- He will speak to the secrets of human hearts.
- He will show the reality of Jesus' ability to recover, restore, and redeem the brokenness of their lives.
- He will demonstrate Jesus' power on the spot and confirm His Word to them.

If we'll simply minister the testimony of the true and living Jesus in the spirit of His love and compassion, the Holy Spirit of prophecy will do the rest. And people will come to Christ—not so persuaded by our reasonings as convinced by the Holy Spirit's making the testimony of Jesus real.

Thus, it seems to me, a dilemma in contemporary evangelism is resolved. Our mission is kept uncluttered. It may still be criticized, but it can't truly be ostracized. There are too many "prophets" being anointed, whose clear mission is directed not at the dissection of other religious systems, but to the declaration of Jesus' Person and Power. Our role is a good news one, not as prophets assigned to condemn the unbelieving to eternal torment, but as commissioned ambassadors proclaiming, "Be reconciled to God."

Two Requirements

However, to be faithful in doing that, the uniqueness of Christ requires two things of me. My *motivation* dare not be passive, and my *message* dare not be unschooled or untargeted. I need to be constrained by a passion about man's lostness and be crystalline in my presentation of the Word, for it is only that impassioned and precisioned testimony of Jesus which the Spirit will confirm.

Constrained by a Passion

When I propose that our mission is not primarily to declare damnation I do *not* mean that eternal loss isn't the consequence of unbelief. Hell's reality is a painful but inescapable truth, an eternal option that must not be forgotten. Incipient doubts, often in the name of Christian enlightenment, have led some to yield to error. Universalism is always afoot and open to acceptance where the uniqueness of Christ is forgotten by the church. Too soon, too many take too lightly that the unsaved will be lost. Too easily people concoct unbiblical systems of salvation for everyone—somehow, sometime, even outside Christ. But however compassionate opposing views may seem, they are blinded efforts at loving, and these blind guides will lead blind souls into the ditch of hopeless loss. Any notion that hell or eternal judgment is an illusion is smashed by the words of Paul:

Knowing, therefore, the terror of the Lord, we persuade men . . . for the love of Christ compels us, because we judge thus: that if One died for all, then all died.

2 Corinthians 5:11, 14

The issue is categorically closed:

Christ died for sin
   because
all are lost through sin
   and shall
forever die in sin
   apart from His salvation.

In this light, the mood of our mission must always be impassioned.

We are ambassadors for Christ, as though God were pleading through us: we implore you on Christ's behalf, be reconciled to God. For He made Him who knew no sin to be sin for us that we might become the righteousness of God in Him.

2 Corinthians 5:20–21

The uniqueness of Christ both constrains and confines me. Though my mission may not be to debunk the systems of a pagan culture, still my manner must never be paralyzed by passivity. Ours is a life-or-death mission—for every person—eternally. It's sobering, gripping, and unforgettable. And it's the truth. A passionate spirit of love for eternal souls must be ever present, and with it, let us be:

Crystalline in Our Presentation

What is the testimony of Jesus we plan to raise if we expect the Holy Spirit to take it and press it to the soul of today's society? I propose that the truth which the spirit of prophecy will most readily anoint is that which simply and pointedly exalts the excellence of Jesus' own person. Accordingly, let us prepare those whom we teach, that they may be equipped with precision-cut, life-begetting words of pure gospel grace and power, crystal pure and unmuddied by speculation or attempted cleverness.

No part of the Bible quite touches John's Gospel for this task. Here, as hardly anywhere else, Christ is revealed to *ignite faith:*

> These [things] are written that you may believe that Jesus is the Christ, the Son of God, and that believing you may have life in His name.
>
> John 20:31

I suggest that the essence of our testimony might be in the same spirit. John proclaimed Jesus to a pagan world without confusion and without condemnation, yet he never lacks clarity or a call to spiritual commitment. Let us take his testimony of Jesus as our model; for example,

- John's testimony of Jesus as the Creator (chapter 1) speaks to a world like ours; steeped in ideas of its amoeba-then-animal derivation, and thereby crawling in its hopelessness. But to this culture, we may proclaim man as the special creation of Christ, our Creator, who has a special plan for each; a plan that transcends the law of the survival of the fittest and affords meaning to hearing hearts.

- See John's testimony of Jesus the Miracle Worker (chapter 2) and note the good news for an empty world, fresh out of wine. Jesus' ability to take the ordinariness of water and turn it to the extraordinariness of wine can do the same with the lives of ordinary people. Let the Holy Spirit of prophecy anoint that testimony to bring extraordinary hope!

Continue with John. See chapter 4's testimony:

- Jesus is the sole satisfaction for immoral people who wait, wearied and thirsty, at the sour cistern of bitter relationships. Jesus is the Living Water they seek—springing up to eternal life. And see chapter 5:

- Jesus is able to meet paralyzed souls at the point of their crippledness, sounding His call: "Get up! In My Name you have a future."

John's Gospel throbs with such positive, buoyant witness—an uplifting, soul-refreshing testimony of Jesus—that it demonstrates a timelessly contemporary message; one we can set forth to assert the Savior's claims without assailing other systems. However, one crucial complement remains.

Of Pivotal Importance

The testimony of Jesus joined to the Spirit of prophecy can only be truly effective when touched by a fresh oil anointing of the Holy Spirit. This is what Jesus was promising as He taught His disciples of the coming of the Comforter, the Holy Spirit. Five times He describes benefits and actions resulting from the Holy Spirit's outpouring on the church, saying, "When He comes . . ."

1. He will abide with you (John 14:16–17).
2. He will teach you (John 14:26).
3. He will testify of Me (John 15:26).
4. He will convince others of My excellence and triumph (John 16:7–11).
5. He will glorify Me (John 16:13–14).

Pivotal for us is the difference between the grammatical form of the first statement above from the following four. Jesus' opening promise—"He will abide with you"—is in the subjunctive, a quali-fier indicating conditions for the Holy Spirit's "abiding." The fol-lowing four are all in the indicative mood, guaranteeing the Holy Spirit's actions. But the four guarantees are predicated upon the first condition! The condition of the Spirit's abiding—His being with us—is the factor which determines the continuing dynamism of our witness.

You and I must grasp the significance of this "hinge" upon which the fullness of the promises' fulfillment turns. Jesus is assuring us that, from His side, the abiding presence of the Spirit of power is available, but on our side, a condition of our welcoming and walking in His pres-ence is essential. It isn't a threat, but simply a contractual fact: The Holy Spirit only abides where He is continually welcomed! He imposes His presence and operations on no one. He is ready, but only where we are willing!

- Only a humble walk in dependence upon His daily en-ablement will bring fruitfulness.

- Only a childlike teachability will ensure His regularly teach-ing us, giving gifts of discernment, knowledge, and wisdom forthcoming.

- Only a fresh fullness borne of intimate times with Him will cause our testimony of Jesus to be borne by the Spirit of prophecy.

- And it is only His present, moment-by-moment abiding that will take your words and mine and make them con-vincing to others and glorifying of Christ—thereby draw-ing all men unto Him.

The condition of the Spirit's presence (not merely the confession of a past experience) is that qualifier we must never forget.

However glorious, the history of our revival in this century will not carry the church into a new millennium, nor will our past experi-ences qualify us for what God has ahead. As individuals joined by a com-mon bond of renewal and awakening, let us today heed Isaiah's prophecy:

> Behold, the former things have come to pass, And new things
> I declare; Before they spring forth I tell you of them.
> Isaiah 42:9

Let us hear it, loved ones. The same Spirit of prophecy waiting to anoint our witness to the testimony of Jesus in all His uniqueness is the One who adds yet this reminder: Your history is no guarantee of your future!

So let us come again, humbly, to Jesus Himself. Let us request of Him a fresh anointing by the Holy Spirit of prophecy. And as we do, He will answer, and our love for Christ and for one another will abound

and the world shall know,

and the lost shall be reached,

and they shall be saved.

And God's purpose in filling us shall be fulfilled—again and again.

Listen, I hear His Spirit seeming to call to me—to all of us—once again:

"When I first called you to be renewed and rekindled in My Spirit's refreshing waters and fires of refinement, I did a new thing. But hear Me, child. Your call is not to endlessly embrace the former thing I have done but to open your arms to tomorrow.

"I am preparing to do a new thing, but it will require a new stance on your part to receive it.

"Remember the uncertainty you felt when you first learned to walk in the Spirit? But you lack that today. You have become too secure in your experience, too self-confident, too "safe" to step into new things. So I say to you:

Humble your heart before Me anew.

Open your soul with a hunger for a yet undiscovered fullness.

Lay aside the accumulated baggage of the journey you have traversed, and stand freed for new direction.

"You do not need a new word from heaven or a new opportunity for labor. You only need a new thing done in your soul . . . and I have come to announce that intent.

"Behold—look up!

"Look to Me, and I will do a new thing that is new in every way . . .

as the new flesh of an infant, I will soften your soul;

as the new light of a dawn, I will bring revelation to My Word; and

as the fragrance of a freshly cut flower, I will bring glory to your new day,

"Look to Me. I tell you, it will spring forth. It will spring forth. It will spring forth!

"The Lord of Creation promises new things. But you must not lean on the former.

"Simply look to Me for the newness of My life springing up in you, and that life will multiply through you.

"As at the first creation, the seas shall swarm with life, and your seed shall inherit the earth, says the Lord. Rise now, child, and receive My newness of working in you."

My message to the conference concluded with that promising summons of God's Spirit. And in its light, dear reader, would you ask yourself: Is this call of our Lord applicable to you as it was to them in Brighton? It would seem so, wouldn't it?

- The Holy Spirit is calling each of us to fullness.

- The world is crying out for an answer to brokenness.

- The promise of God's Word does offer all of us renewal in His life and power.

I've described to you how I first answered the call to open to the loveliness of the Holy Spirit's working by simply drawing nearer to the heart of God. That pursuit occasioned far more than the discovery of the beauty of spiritual language, it opened to the liberty of a renewed spiritual lifestyle. It's a way for us all—a way of life marked by love, joy, peace, and soundmindedness. And the grandest fact of all is that it carries within itself the seeds of multiplying that loving, joyful, peace-ministering life to others.

The morning after addressing the great congress, I was walking near the hotel just before preparing to return home to Los Angeles. The pier that had so captured my thoughts two days before lay there to my left as I slowed my pace and stopped to read a memorial. Directly across the street from the remains of the shore-side entrance to South Pier, a grassy rise provides a picnic spot for beach visitors. Apparently, years before, a stone monument had been placed at the park's entrance. Its inscription read:

> To the Officers and Men of the Royal Sussex
> Regiment fallen in Africa, 1900–1902 A.D.

Somehow that memorial, along with the dilapidated pier, summarized both the fleeting fancies of mankind, on the one hand, and his certain demise, on the other.

But between the two, a bright boulevard invited the traveler past the pier and beyond the monument. I looked up and smiled as I again read the highway's name on the sign which pointed hopefully—beyond the rubble of the pier and past the ruin marked by the monument. The avenue was named *Kingsway!*

I laughed for joy, and I praised the King. For it's His Way—Christ's alone—that is still the path to life and glory.

And it's your highway and mine, loved one. A highway of hope, holiness, and holy power for living. It's ours to walk with Him and with one another. And it's ours to share with others how the beauty of Christ's life and love can fill their hopes and heal their hurt.

And its the beauty of His Spirit's abiding fullness and enabling that will make *us* sufficient to present *His* all sufficiency to *them*—sufficiently!

Appendix 1

Receiving Christ as Lord and Savior

It seems possible that some earnest inquirer may have read this book and somehow still never have received Jesus Christ as personal Savior. If that's true of you, that you have never personally welcomed the Lord Jesus into your heart, to be your Savior and to lead you in the matters of your life, I would like to encourage and help you to do that.

There is no need to delay, for an honest heart can approach the loving Father God at any time. So I'd like to invite you to come with me, and let's pray to Him right now.

If it's possible there where you are, bow your head, or even kneel if you can. In either case, let me pray a simple prayer first and then I've added words for you to pray yourself.

My Prayer

Father God, I have the privilege of joining with this child of Yours who is reading this book right now. I want to thank You for the openness of heart being shown toward You and I want to praise You for Your promise, that when we call to You, You will answer.

I know that genuine sincerity is present in this heart, which is ready to speak this prayer, and so we come to You in the Name and through the Cross of Your Son, the Lord Jesus. Thank You for hearing. (And now, speak your prayer.)

Your Prayer

Dear God, I am doing this because I believe in Your love for me, and I want to ask You to come to me as I come to You. Please help me now.

First, I thank You for sending Your Son Jesus to earth to live and to die for me on the Cross. I thank you for the gift of forgiveness of sin that You offer me now, and I pray for that forgiveness.

Do, I pray, forgive me and cleanse my life in Your sight, through the blood of Jesus Christ. I am sorry for anything and everything I have ever done that is unworthy in Your sight. Please take away all guilt and shame as I accept the fact that Jesus died to pay for all my sins, and through Him I am now given forgiveness on this earth and eternal life in heaven.

I ask You, Lord Jesus, please come into my life now. Because You rose from the dead, I know You're alive and I want You to live with me—now and forever.

I am turning my life over to You and turning from my way to Yours. I invite Your Holy Spirit to fill me and lead me forward in a life that will please the heavenly Father.

Thank You for hearing me. From this day forward, I commit myself to Jesus Christ the Son of God. In His name, amen.[1]

Appendix 2

A Prayer for Inviting the Lord to Fill You with the Holy Spirit

Dear Lord Jesus,

I thank You and praise You for Your great love and faithfulness to me.

My heart is filled with joy whenever I think of the great gift of salvation You have so freely given to me,

And I humbly glorify You, Lord Jesus,

for You have forgiven me all my sins and brought me to the Father.

Now I come in obedience to Your call.

I want to receive the fullness of the Holy Spirit.

I do not come because I am worthy myself, but because You have invited me to come.

Because You have washed me from my sins,

I thank You that You have made the vessel of my life a worthy one to be filled with the Holy Spirit of God.

I want to be overflowed with Your life,

Your love and Your power, Lord Jesus.

I want to show forth Your grace,

Your Words,

Your goodness, and

Your gifts

to everyone I can.

And so with simple, childlike faith, I ask You, Lord,

Fill me with the Holy Spirit.

> I open all of myself to You,
>   to receive all of Yourself in me.
> I love You, Lord, and I lift my voice in praise to You.
> I welcome Your might and Your miracles
>   to be manifested in me
>   for Your glory
>   and unto Your praise.

I don't tell people to say amen at the end of this prayer, because after inviting Jesus to fill you, it is good to begin to praise Him in faith. Praisefully worship Jesus and simply allow the Holy Spirit to help you do so. He will manifest Himself in a Christ-glorifying way, and you can ask Him to enrich this moment by causing you to know the presence and power of the Lord Jesus. Don't hesitate to expect the same things in your experience as occurred to people in the Bible. The spirit of praise is an appropriate way to express that expectation, and to make Jesus your focus, worship as you praise. Glorify Him and leave the rest to the Holy Spirit.[1]

The following poem was sent to me by a radio listener who later wrote that she had received the fullness of the Holy Spirit *and* a release in spiritual language. It's a simple, lovely expression of the kind of "hunger and thirst for righteousness" that finds fullness in Christ.

Dear Spirit of God,

> I read the Book of Acts today
> And now my heart is shaken
> For I know not how to understand
> Yet my heart has been awakened.
>
> It said they waited for You to come
> To fill them in that hour
> And as a mighty rushing wind
> You came in all Your power.
>
> With tongues that danced upon their heads
> They spoke with boldness loud
> In foreign languages they had never known
> As they ministered to the crowd.
>
> And the Book of Acts continued
> As You entered so many more

And they too were empowered and spoke in tongues
In which no one had heard before.

Oh Holy Spirit, please understand
I feel a draw toward You
But I've been told that not all receive *tongues*
And to keep from those who do.

I believe Your Word, and what it says:
That You'll always be the same.
But I've been coached "charismatics are just
    emotional";
That *tongues* "are just their game."

I need more than games within my life
To help me fight the foe
To not only defeat the enemy
But to help my spirit grow.

Yet I know that there's got to be something more
To this life I've tried to live
And that God wouldn't leave me to fight alone—
There must be more He'll give.

Oh Holy Spirit, I choose to not listen
To what other men may say
It is Your turn now . . . please speak to me
You show me how to pray.

Susan Cook

Appendix 3

Singing Spiritual Songs

There are wide differences in definitions of spiritual songs, and I don't want to appear either ignorant or critical of any of them. But it seems clear that spiritual songs were the apostle Paul's reference to a distinct music form unique to the church. It was one which would help fulfill the prospect of God's wanting to give everyone their own song of praise to Him.

Spiritual songs have sometimes been defined as informal choruses, choral anthems, simpler, more personal statements of faith or brief, uncomplex odes of worship. But I propose that they were—and are—a new music form unavailable until the New Testament, until Christ's full redemption allowed the Holy Spirit to dwell in mankind. Clearly, early believers sang spiritual songs of worship. But what were they?

Hodais pneumatikais, the exact words in both Ephesians 5 and Colossians 3, is usually translated "spiritual songs."[1] The first word is simply "ode," the Greek term for any words which were sung. But the second word—*pneumatikais*—seems to be the key to the full meaning of this phrase.

Pneumatikais—a cognate of *pneuma* ("spirit")—is most easily defined and understood noting its use elsewhere in the New Testament. For example, Paul uses this word when introducing the subject of spiritual gifts in 1 Corinthians 12:1 (literally, *pneumatika,* "spiritual things"). Later in his appeal to the Galatians concerning their duty to restore fallen brethren, the word also appears: "You who are spiritual ones" (*pneumatikoi*) are assigned the task of that restoring ministry.

Although *pneumatika* occurs more than twenty times in the New Testament, those two texts give us something of a basic picture. *Pneumatika* seems to indicate Holy-Spirit-filled people of character and charisma: Their character is noted in the Galatian text: "you who are spiritual ones restore the fallen"; their *charism* (in the sense of their functioning in the charisms—gifts of the Holy Spirit) is indicated in their apparent acceptance and response to spiritual things; that is, manifestations of the Holy Spirit's gifts (1 Cor. 12:7).

These factors alone would not finalize a definition, except for the fact that in this same context Paul discusses "singing with the spirit and with the understanding." It is here in this classic passage, 1 Corinthians 12–14, as the apostle corrects their abuse of glossolalia, that he also discusses singing of a distinctly Holy-Spirit-enabled nature:

> For if I pray in a tongue, my spirit prays, but my understanding is unfruitful. What is the result then? I will pray with the spirit, and I will also pray with the understanding. I will sing with the spirit, and I will also sing with the understanding.
>
> 1 Corinthians 14:14–15

His distinguishing singing "with the spirit" from "singing with the understanding" points to what spiritual songs may have meant in the first-century church: an exercise separate from yet complementary to the singing of psalms and hymns.

Since the general passage beginning in 1 Corinthians 12:1 and the specific text beginning in 1 Corinthians 14:1 both use *pneumatika* to describe the kind of subject matter being dealt with, it follows that the distinct type of singing referred to as being "with the spirit (*pneuma*)" could be the same as spiritual songs. I would not be so bigoted as to oppose another interpretation, but I propose that the whole of the New Testament context supports the definition of spiritual songs as being Holy-Spirit-enabled utterances:

- which were sung rather than spoken
- which were most commonly to be a part of one's devotional life
- which were explained or interpreted if exercised in corporate gatherings

- which were so desirable as to have Paul assert his personal will to practice them—"I *will* sing with the spirit" (1 Cor. 14:15, emphasis added)

I would not preclude the possibility or desirability of spiritual songs being in the native language of the worshiper nor suggest that one (glossolalia or native tongue) was preferable to another. But it does seem clear that the Holy Spirit is at work in this worship expression, doing something distinctly valid and valuable.[2]

Appendix 4

The Bible and the Term "Spiritual Language"

In writing this book, I'm using the more contemporary term "spiritual language" for the simple reason that it's an easier way to describe speaking with tongues. Even though "tongues" is a biblical expression, it tends to conjure up strange images in people's minds:

- Images of uncontrolled speech or incoherent, babbling ecstasy
- A voodoo-like mumbo-jumbo muttered from slightly foaming lips
- Weird gibberish emitted from a stiffened body besieged by hypnotic trance

This problem is compounded by the fact that in the most technical terms, all of the above are described as "ecstatic speech," an expression often used for biblical tongue speaking. Let's correct this idea first of all.

May I begin by establishing the fact that the term "ecstasy" is never associated with tongue speakers in the Bible. Erstwhile observers, ardent adherents, and animated antagonists of spiritual language all have used the term "ecstatic speech" for "tongues," but it isn't biblical. Early in my ministry I did the same, supposing that "ecstatic utterance" lent something of dignity to the Maker of speaking with tongues, but a proper definition shows that this is as unsound an idea as it is unscriptural. The primary dictionary definition for *ecstasy* is: "A state of being beyond reason and self-control through intense emotional excitement, pain or other sensation."[1] Now, I have seen a lot of people very happy and even "excited" after they experienced the Spirit's rivers of living water overflowing their soul. But their exercise of spiritual language wasn't a case of losing control. Neither was their joyous experience fomented by a fanning of emotions used to induce speaking with tongues. Control may be surrendered to the Holy Spirit, but it isn't cast into the air or abandoned by succumbing to some state of mindless oblivion.

Now, Webster's second definition for "ecstasy"—"exalted, rapturous delight"[2]—frankly does touch something which Holy-Spirit-fullness often produces, and since speaking with tongues often attends breakthrough experiences of divine blessing, a biblical delight may be expected.

> In Your presence is fullness of joy;
> At Your right hand are pleasures forevermore.
> Psalm 16:11

> Though now you do not see Him, yet believing, you rejoice with joy inexpressible and full of glory.
> 1 Peter 1:8

> For the kingdom of God is . . . righteousness and peace and joy in the Holy Spirit.
> Romans 14:17

Moments of joyfulness or warm emotion are certainly present at times with most who humbly and openly enter the Savior's presence in worship; however, "uncontrollable" is *far* from the mark. I want to emphasize what the Bible says in this regard, because fear of the "uncontrollable" or of "manipulated emotions" is enough to discourage most inquirers by distorting the image of a healthy, ongoing experience of spiritual language.

Curiously enough, however, the association of "ecstasy" to "tongues" is probably due to the fact that this word's root does appear in Acts 2:12, within the narrative of the Holy Spirit's visitation at Pentecost:

> So they were all amazed [*eksistanto*] and perplexed, saying to one another, "Whatever could this mean?"

The Greek verb *eksistemi* (from which we derive "ecstasy" in English) is here, but please notice it isn't used of the ones who spoke with tongues; it's used of the observers! And it was their amazement (ecstasy) which prompted their inquiry about tongues speaking: "What is this?" Note, then, that the spiritual language spoken by the believers, while certainly joy-inducing, was *not* the thing described as ecstatic. Rather, the stunned, ecstatic response was the impact realized by the unbelieving crowd looking on.

In denying the use of "ecstasy" as often misconstrued, I hasten to say that I am not arguing for a limp, lifeless experience of the Holy Spirit's wonder working. But I make this point because inaccurate descriptions of the experience of spiritual language have spooked people away. Perhaps a less mysticized understanding might help more toward a ready personal availability to spiritual language in their own lives.

Further, to use the expression "spiritual language" as a more easily accepted description of tongues speaking is precisely biblical. A look into the epistles shows this, because references to tongues here are more expansively dealt with than in Acts. They show Holy-Spirit-assisted language as positively applicable in prayer or praise. Tongues are said to be (1) "speaking to God" (1 Cor. 14:2), and (2) as "giving thanks" (1 Cor. 14:16–17). The apostle Paul also speaks very approvingly of these languages for use in devotion as well as in adoration (1 Cor. 14:5a, 18). Notice his terminology in describing his own practice: "I will pray with the spirit . . . I will sing with the spirit" (1 Cor 14:15); terms similar to those he uses in encouraging all believers to do the same.

> Sustain a continuous fullness in the Spirit . . . [with] *spiritual* songs, singing and making melody in your heart to the Lord.[3]
> Ephesians 5:18–19

> Take the whole armor of God . . . [and] stand therefore, having been girded . . . praying always with all prayer and supplication *in the Spirit.*[4]
> Ephesians 6:11–18

The expression "spiritual language" is derived from such references where speaking or singing with tongues is described. The phrases "filled with the Spirit" (Eph. 5:18) and "praying . . . in the Spirit" (Eph. 6:18) are the same in the biblical Greek—*en pneumati.* This phrase literally means, "in the spiritual realm and with the Holy Spirit's aid." In

Paul's encouragement to sing "spiritual songs" (Eph. 5:19), the word *pneumatikos* ("spiritual") he uses is defined as "pertaining or relating to the influences of the Holy Spirit, superior in process to the natural course of things, miraculous."[5]

These texts show how accurately—and biblically—prayer and praise which speaks or sings in tongues may properly be described as using "spiritual language," because the root "spirit" (*pneuma*) is common to the words used in describing tongues. Of course, using the word "spiritual" for this prayer language isn't to suggest that spoken prayer or praise in one's native language is unspiritual or semispiritual. Each form of prayer is at a different dimension, and neither should be described as "less than." How can the Grand Canyon and the Swiss Alps be compared? It's impossible and unnecessary to do so. Rather, be it languages we employ or creation we behold, let us all be humbled before all manifestations of His Majesty's glory. Let us rise together to praise the Creator of all prayer as readily as we worship the Creator of all things. To do so is to be open to experiencing the enjoyment and the blessing available in exploring the dimensions to which each realm invites us.

Notes

Chapter 1 • *The Beauty of Spiritual Language*

1. Leann Payne, *The Healing Presence* (Wheaton, Ill.: Crossway Books, 1989)

Chapter 3 • *Love's Language of Praise*

1. The call was fulfilled. My sister eventually went into mission work. She later died of cancer during her service as a missionary to Hong Kong.
2. Charles Wesley, "O for a Thousand Tongues."
3. Samuel Medley, "O Could I Speak Thy Matchless Worth."
4. Bernard of Clairvaux, "O Sacred Head Now Wounded."
5. Emphasis mine.

Chapter 4 • *Though I Speak with Tongues*

1. Adrian Plass, *Diary* (London: Marshall, Morgan, and Scott, 1987), 72.
2. From my notes of one of Joe Blinco's Bible studies given at one of the Foursquare Church's International Conventions in the 1970s.

Chapter 5 • *The Light Coming from Above*

1. Jamie Buckingham, *Summer of Miracles* (Altamonte Springs, Fla.: Creation House, 1991), 82. Used by permission.
2. Ibid., 95.

Chapter 6 • *Historic Landmarks—Broadening Boundaries*

1. To my view, they deserve the same respect we give the pilgrims who settled early America. They bore the price of suffering and the onus of rejection for spiritual convictions, and they pioneered a new era in church history. A study of church history over the past century confirms the impact of their will to "pioneer."

2. Gerhard Kittel and Gerhard Friedrich, eds., *Theological Dictionary of the New Testament*, 10 vols. (Grand Rapids, Mich.: Eerdmans, 1964–76), s.v. *thelo*.

3. Sometimes people ask, "If you say tongues are for everybody because all at Pentecost received the spiritual language, then shouldn't you also expect that the divided tongues of fire should also be expected today?" This is a reasonable question but inconsistent with the point. Both of the other two miraculous signs—the rushing mighty wind and divided tongues upon each head were neither signs involving a conscious participation of the praying band of Christians. With regard to the spiritual language, and as we have noted, *they* spoke. Further, the spiritual language *does* recur in a positive context among believers after Pentecost, whereas the two other manifestations do not.

4. This reference cannot be passed without addressing the fact that a small sector of the church today, resistant to the contemporaneity of the Holy Spirit's gifts, signs, and wonders, have posited "when that which is perfect is come" (1 Cor. 13:10) to refer to the completion of the canon of the New Testament Scriptures. In other words, the argument goes, these signs and gifts were only immature expressions of God's working; when the text of the Scriptures came to a conclusion (near the end of the first century), then all this immaturity ceased.

Lest some readers suppose that rejection of this view is only the opinion of pentecostals or charismatics, a sampling of the prevailing opinions of other scholars is cited here, showing the "perfect" to come clearly refers to the Second Coming of our Lord Jesus Christ.

R. C. H. Lenski observed, "The aorist subjunctive *elthe* marks the great future moment when the goal shall be reached, namely the Parousia of Christ" (*The Interpretation of St. Paul's First and Second Epistles to the Corinthians* [Minneapolis, Minn.: Augsburg, 1937], 566).

F. W. Grosheide wrote: "[these words refer to a time] when the zenith has been reached. . . . All things hasten to the end, to the culmination point; the Christian must reckon with that fact. Once the acme has been reached and this dispensation comes to an end, then all that belonged to this dispensation, including the charismata, will terminate" (*The First Epistle to the Corinthians,* The International Commentary on the New Testament [Grand Rapids, Mich.: Eerdmans, 1953], 309–10. In related notes, Grosheide uses 1 Corinthians 7:31 and 15:25 to explain that by "this dispensation" he is referring to the church age, which will conclude at Christ's Second Coming.

Henry Alford noted, "unquestionably the time alluded to is that of the coming of the Lord" (*The New Testament for English Readers* [Chicago: Moody Press, n.d.], 1058).

Heinrich Meyer concluded, "Both [tongues and prophecy] contain only fragments of the great whole which remains hidden from us as such *before* the Parousia [i.e., Christ's Second Coming]; . . . [but] with the advent of the absolute the imperfect finite ceases to exist, as the dawn ceases after the rising of the sun. . . . What Paul means and says is that these charismata . . . will cease to exist at the Parousia" (*Critical and Exegetical Handbook to the Epistle to the Corinthians* [New York: Funk and Wagnalls, 1894], 305).

Far more scholarship may be marshalled to verify the point, but this extended note should be sufficient to assure any inquirer that the notion touted by a vocal few that "the perfect" has always been taken to mean "the Scriptures when concluded" is by no means a preponderant opinion.

Chapter 7 • *For You May All Prophesy*

1. From the *Spirit-Filled Life Bible* (Nashville, Tenn.: Thomas Nelson, 1991), 210, comment on Num. 11:29.

Chapter 8 • *A Beauty with Blessed Benefits*

1. Paul quotes the preceding verse, Isa. 28:11, but the contextual relationship seems to be as clear in noting the tongues as an instrument of "rest . . . refreshing," as well as being a sign to the unbeliever.

Chapter 9 • *For the Promise Is to You*

1. See Appendix 1 article on receiving Christ as Lord and Savior.
2. See Appendix 3 on singing spiritual songs.

Chapter 10 • *The Ultimate Beauty—The Uniqueness of Christ*

1. This copy, prepared for publication in this book, is structured somewhat differently from the original. Each conference message was interpreted into one of four official conference languages. Because of the undesirability of listening to a sermon with phrase-to-phrase interruptions of interpretation in another language, I later recorded this message on an occasion I delivered it at the Church on the Way from this written text.

Appendix 1 • *Receiving Christ as Lord and Savior*

1. Partially excerpted from Jack Hayford, *I'll Hold You in Heaven* (Ventura, Calif.: Regal Books, 1990), 38–39.

Appendix 2 • A Prayer for Inviting the Lord to Fill You with the Holy Spirit

1. Excerpt taken from Jack Hayford, *Spirit-Filled* (Wheaton, Ill.: Tyndale House Publishers, 1988), 50–51. Used by permission.

Appendix 3 • Singing Spiritual Songs

1. Both the *Living Bible* and *Today's English Version* read "sacred songs," but the New International, New English, New King James, Revised Standard, Phillips, and the older King James Version all translate to "spiritual songs."
2. Excerpt from Jack W. Hayford, *Worship His Majesty* (Waco, Tex.: Word Books, 1987), 150–52. Used by permission.

Appendix 4 • The Bible and the Term "Spiritual Language"

1. *Webster's Third International Dictionary,* s.v. "ecstasy."
2. Ibid.
3. Emphasis and paraphrase mine.
4. Emphasis and paraphrase mine.
5. *Harper's Analytical Greek Lexicon,* s.v. "*pneumatikos.*"